Piers Plowman Studies VI

# NATURE AND SALVATION IN PIERS PLOWMAN

Piers Plowman Studies

I  THE THEME OF GOVERNMENT IN PIERS PLOWMAN
Anna Baldwin

II  THE FIGURE OF PIERS PLOWMAN
Margaret E. Goldsmith

III  PERSONIFICATION IN PIERS PLOWMAN
Lavinia Griffiths

IV  THE CLERKLY MAKER:
LANGLAND'S POETIC ART
A. V. C. Schmidt

V  PIERS PLOWMAN:
A GLOSSARY OF LEGAL DICTION
John A. Alford

# Nature and Salvation in Piers Plowman

## HUGH WHITE

D. S. BREWER

© Hugh White 1988

First published 1988 by D. S. Brewer
240 Hills Road, Cambridge
an imprint of Boydell & Brewer Ltd
PO Box 9, Woodbridge, Suffolk IP12 3DF
and of Boydell & Brewer Inc.
Wolfeboro, New Hampshire 03894-2069, USA

ISBN 0 85991 271 X


British Library Cataloguing in Publication Data

White, Hugh
    Nature and salvation in Piers Plowman.——
    (Piers Plowman studies, 6).
    1. Poetry in English. Langland, William.
    Piers Plowman. Characters: Piers Plowman –
    Critical studies
    I. Title      II. Series
    821'.1
    ISBN 0-85991-271-X


Library of Congress Cataloging-in-Publication Data

White, Hugh.
    Nature and salvation in Piers Plowman / Hugh White.
        p.      cm. — (Piers Plowman studies ; 6)
    Bibliography: p.
    ISBN 0-85991-271-X (alk. paper)
    1. Langland, William, 1330?–1400? Piers the Plowman.   2. Nature
in literature.   3. Salvation in literature.   I. Title.   II. Series.
PR2017.N38W47   1988
821'.1—dc19                                              88-14518
                                                        CIP

♾ Printed on long life paper
made to the full American Standard

Printed in Great Britain by
St Edmundsbury Press, Bury St Edmunds, Suffolk

# Contents

for Carolinne

*'cor unum, anima una'*

## Acknowledgements

I am pleased to acknowledge the great debt this book owes to Dr Malcolm Godden, who supervised the thesis on which it draws and who supplied helpful advice unsparingly as it took its present shape.

I wrote the book while at the University of the Witwatersrand, Johannesburg, and I should like to acknowledge financial assistance towards its composition received from that institution. I should also like to thank my former colleagues in the Department of English there for their companionship at a time when we were all in a position to feel something of what it was like to be inside the beleaguered Unity Holy Church. In particular, I would express my gratitude to Dr Jan Gorak and Mr Timothy Trengove-Jones, who read and commented on part of this work and who on all occasions offered much stimulation and encouragement.

London, 1988                                                                                    HRBW

# Introduction

In various different manifestations the concept *kynde* plays a highly significant role in *Piers Plowman* in all versions of the poem.[1] Perhaps most strikingly, God is identified as Kynde in the second part of the poem, but Langland also makes great play of the concept of *kynde wit* and the idea of knowing *kyndely*.[2] Further, being *kynde* turns out to be a highly important moral desiderandum, perhaps the most important, and Langland has his Samaritan offer a dense and lengthy exposition of the idea.

It seems to me that Langland is determined to have the natural an important agent in man's salvation, perhaps because, at root, he optimistically conceives the basic situation and capacities of man to be attuned to that end. This optimism, if such it is, has to encounter the corrosive effects of Langland's unillusioned honesty, of a realism which renders the ideal structures the poet's hope bodies forth extremely unstable. The poem proceeds by questioning its own solutions and revising what had looked like its conclusions. Langland's understanding of the operations of the natural is caught up in this process of reformulation; the positive nature of its influence is seen to be questionable, its benignity discovered to be by no means self-evident. Nevertheless, Langland's conviction of the importance and goodness of the natural is able to stand these stresses. Indeed, towards the end of the poem the idea of *kynde*ness becomes a locus for intimations of a coming together of human and divine, and the divine itself is seen as constrained by the *kynde*.

One of the reasons why the *kynde* can function so importantly for Langland is that *kynde* and related terms have a great semantic richness. Nature is one of the more polysemous words in Modern English, and it can be argued that Middle English *kynde* was even more so, since its field included not only the idea of nature but also the idea of kindness, which modern nature terms do not cover. This extreme polysemy, a resource for Langland, is something of an impediment to the critic; it is not always easy

---

[1] There are some indications, to which I shall advert, that Langland became less enthusiastic about the natural in C than he was in B, though the natural still retains enormous significance and power in C.

[2] I consider *kynde wit* and *kynde knowynge* to be different concepts. See Chapter 2.

*1*

to know what meaning of *kynde* is operative, even before one starts to make allowances for the possibility of word-play, Langland's propensity for which is well-established.[3] This necessitates in what follows much rather intricate investigation of what Langland may be meaning at particular junctures, and certain resolution of the difficulties encountered here is not always possible.

The polysemy of *kynde* also threatens any divisions one employs in a treatment of the subject of the natural in *Piers Plowman*. Nevertheless, certain divisions, which I have, in fact, already used in the first paragraph, do seem legitimate tools, and I shall move from considerations of *kynde wit* and *kynde knowynge* through an examination of the figure of Kynde, to a discussion of what it is to be *kynde* and *unkynde* in Langland's eyes. These divisions give some structure to the discussion, but I have not neglected the interconnections between these different areas, through which, it seems to me, some of Langland's most pleasing and profound suggestions are made.

I have not pursued Langland's conceptions with any great determination into the literary and theological backgrounds, though I do discuss possible indebtedness to, for instance, legal understandings of the natural and the Chartrian presentation of Nature.[4] Langland is very much his own writer, and though it is possible to suggest a provenance for some of his notions, this kind of endeavour very soon exposes one to the risk (and temptation) of imposing the shape of alien contexts on Langland's text. With a poet as unpredictable as Langland the application of context has to be handled with considerable delicacy, and the primary obligation must be to acknowledge the complexities of the text itself, avoiding ironing these out in order to be able to impose a pattern derived from elsewhere.[5] Indeed, because I take Langland to be a poet not securely in control of his material and his poem to show signs of this lack of control, of, perhaps we might say, its unachieved condition, I do not seek to produce a neat interpretative schema, but rather to indicate certain directions in which the text seems to be moving and certain positions towards which it seems to be making perhaps not wholly articulate gestures.

---

[3] See, for instance, B. F. Huppé, '*Petrus id est Christus*: Word Play in *Piers Plowman*, The B-Text', *ELH* 17 (1950), 163–90 and A. V. C. Schmidt, '*Lele Wordes* and *Bele Paroles*: Some Aspects of Langland's Word-Play', *RES*, n.s. 34 (1983), 137–50.

[4] I use the designation Chartrian to refer to a certain literary tradition in a manner now, I think, conventional enough, in spite of the doubt cast on the connections of this tradition with Chartres by R. W. Southern in 'Humanism and the School of Chartres', *Medieval Humanism and Other Studies* (Oxford, 1970), pp. 61–85. For this literary tradition see, e.g., G. D. Economou, *The Goddess Natura in Medieval Literature* (Cambridge, Mass., 1972).

[5] This is not to deny that studies investigating Langland's relations to various traditions of thought can be highly suggestive regarding the workings of Langland's text.

## Chapter One

# Kynde Wit

Kynde wit is a concept of great and abiding significance for Langland. He conceives it as a force for good (though problems develop) and involves it at a fundamental level in several of the structures which he offers as the groundings of the good life. So, for instance, *kynde wit* is a crucial factor in the institution of society described in the B and C Prologues and it directs the society of Christian fools at the end of the poem to dig the moat Holiness. In addition, the poem's great figure of goodness, Piers, is characterised on his first appearance as one guided by Conscience and Kynde Wit. In fact, it is through Conscience and Kynde Wit that Piers has come to know Truth *kyndely*.[1]

The importance of *kynde wit* is clear then, but critics have been divided as to what it means. Skeat suggests 'Common Sense', Tolkien '(natural) good sense'. Dunning, holding both these to be inadequate, thinks that Kynde Wit is practically equivalent to Reason. He supposes Kynde Wit in A denotes the *ratio practica*, the moral faculty.[2] This can be seen as a refinement on the

---

[1] In the B and C versions, that is. A at this point reads

> Clene consience & wyt kende me to his place.

(A VI 27)

Z, however, has 'kynde wit'. Unless otherwise stated my textual references are to G. Kane, *Piers Plowman, The A Version* (London, 1960); A. V. C. Schmidt, *The Vision of Piers Plowman, A Complete Edition of the B Text*, New Edition (London, 1987); Derek Pearsall, *Piers Plowman, An Edition of the C-Text* (London, 1978). The Z text has been edited by A. G. Rigg and Charlotte Brewer (Toronto, 1983).

[2] W. W. Skeat, *The Vision of William concerning Piers the Plowman* (Oxford, 1886; repr. 1954), note on C 1 141 (Pearsall, Prologue 141), Vol. II p. 14; J. R. R. Tolkien, *A Middle English Vocabulary* (Glossary to K. Sisam, ed., *Fourteenth Century Verse and Prose*) (Oxford, 1922), under 'Wit'; T. P. Dunning, *Piers Plowman: An Interpretation of the A-text* 1st ed. (London, 1937), p. 39.

In *The Articulate Citizen and the English Renaissance* (Durham, N.C., 1965) A. B. Ferguson sees *kynde wit* as 'the natural wisdom, the common sense of man by means of which he makes the practical adjustments necessary to civil society' (p. 73). This emphasis on society is quite proper, as will become evident, but when Ferguson suggests that Kynde Wit's vision, unless 'informed by a higher authority, an absolute sense of right' (such as Conscience and Reason possess) is 'limited to the exigencies of the immediate situation' he underestimates the moral authority of Kynde Wit.

'natural reason' offered by several critics. In contrast, Robertson and Huppé, propose *scientia* (which is concerned only with *temporalia*) and speculative intellect,[3] but Schmidt glosses Kynde Wit at B Prologue 114 'Native Intelligence' and explains that Kynde Wit refers to 'natural and practical reason as opposed to speculative intellect'.[4] Pearsall says that Kynde Wit is 'the inborn gift of intelligence, unillumined by divine revelation. . . . Animals have a share in it . . ., and it is the basis of all human knowledge and wisdom . . .'.[5] Frank takes Kynde Wit as 'natural intelligence and what can be learned by the exercise of natural intelligence'.[6] Dunning further identifies Kynde Wit as *synderesis*,[7] whilst Hort sees Kynde Wit, 'Common Wit', as an allegorical presentation of the *lex naturalis*.[8] Quirk claims a scholastic equivalent for *kynde wit* in the *vis cogitativa* which corresponds to the *vis aestimativa* in animals. He sets this against Wit, the *ratio particularis*; the two 'conveniently express these two aspects of the same faculty: *quod bonum est tenete* and *wit wolle the wisse*'.[9] Harwood refines on Quirk's view, seeing the substance of *kynde wit* as the knowledge of material benefit; *kynde wit* is tied to the physical *bonum*.[10] Perhaps the least dignified view of Kynde Wit is that of Jones who associates it with the simple deliverances of the senses which are worked on subsequently by Ymaginatif.[11]

[3] D. W. Robertson, Jr and B. F. Huppé, *Piers Plowman and Scriptural Tradition* (Princeton, 1951), pp. 27, 76, 152. Reviewing this work in *Speculum*, 27 (1952), 245–9, M. W. Bloomfield points out that *scientia* and speculative intellect are by no means identical and suggests that Robertson and Huppé confuse the practical and speculative intellects when discussing Kynde Wit. See also R. Quirk, 'Langland's Use of *Kind Wit* and *Inwit*', *JEGP*, 52 (1953), 183–8 (p. 183, n. 6).

[4] Schmidt (1987) p. 306. It is the practical reason that is involved in making moral decisions. P. M. Kean, 'Love, Law, and *Lewte* in *Piers Plowman*', *RES*, n.s. 15 (1964), 241–61, claims (p. 243, n. 2) that *kynde wit* involves knowledge of right and wrong and is therefore closer in meaning to modern Conscience than to modern Reason (as also is Langland's Reason). Schmidt (1987) glosses *kynde wit* differently elsewhere, e.g. as 'common sense' at B XIV 125 (p. 167).

[5] Pearsall (1978) on C Prologue 141, p. 37.

[6] R. W. Frank, Jr, *Piers Plowman and the Scheme of Salvation* (New Haven, 1957), pp. 63–4.

[7] T. P. Dunning, *Piers Plowman: An Interpretation of the A Text* 2nd ed., revised and edited by T. P. Dolan (Oxford, 1980), p. 26. On *synderesis*, that within man which guarantees, even in the sinner, an attachment to the sovereign good, see O. Lottin, *Psychologie et Morale au XIIe et XIIIe siècles* (Louvain/Gembloux, 1942–60), Vol. II, pp. 103–349; T. C. Potts, *Conscience in Medieval Philosophy* (Cambridge, 1980); the same author's chapter on Conscience in the *Cambridge History of Later Medieval Philosophy* ed. N. Kretzmann, A. Kenny and J. Pinborg (Cambridge, 1982), pp. 687–704; the entry in the *Dictionnaire de Théologie Catholique* ed. A. Vacant and E. Mangenot (Paris, 1903–72).

[8] Greta Hort, *Piers Plowman and Contemporary Religious Thought* (London, 1938), pp. 69–72.

[9] Quirk (1953), p. 185. Quirk reviews the use of terms similar to *kynde wit* in certain other medieval writers. For Kynde Wit and *quod bonum est tenete* see below.

[10] Britton J. Harwood, 'Langland's *Kynde Wit*', *JEGP*, 75 (1976), 330–6. Harwood, modifying Quirk, regards *kynde wit* in men as not innate or instinctual since 'what it knows is something learnable' (p. 331).

[11] H. S. V. Jones, 'Imaginatif in *Piers Plowman*', *JEGP*, 13 (1914) 583–8 (p. 583).

Several of these more or less conflicting definitions might be admissible at different points in the text; the trouble arises when a definition established in the light of a particular passage or passages is taken as universally applicable to Langland's usage. For instance, 'Common Sense', 'natural good sense' and 'practical reason' do not seem to fit the uses of *kynde wit* in the Ymaginatif sequence of the poem, where it has to do with the acquisition of knowledge of physical phenomena and might be considered at least in part a kind of *scientia*, arising out of a speculation on the things of this temporal realm.[12] Even here though, there is reason to grant *kynde wit*, in addition to its knowledge of physical phenomena, a moral scope, a scope which, as Dunning and Quirk, for instance, see, is essential to the concept, and for this reason Robertson and Huppé's definition is untenable.[13] Robertson and Huppé and other critics attempt to establish a relationship between Langland's term and medieval academic usage, but it is not clear that Langland's term is stable enough to permit the location of a single precise equivalent, or, indeed, to allow any very tight definition which will be appropriate in all instances. So when Pearsall's informative note speaks of Kynde Wit as 'unillumined by divine revelation' we should pause to recollect Kynde Wit's apparent awareness of Christian apocalyptic predictions and to reflect on Piers' reference to Christian truths in his account of the path to Truth, a path taught him by Conscience and Kynde Wit. Yet it is certainly true that at points *kynde wit* is seen as 'unillumined by divine revelation'.[14]

This is to suggest that any single definition of *kynde wit* one might offer would need to be rather open, so that all Langland's various usages could be covered. Frank's definition has an appropriate openness and inclusiveness. It correctly makes allowance, for instance, for *kynde wit*'s capacity to mean a faculty or a body of knowledge. Langland's usage is often equivocal in this respect, and there are few passages in which one can be sure that one is dealing simply with the faculty or simply with the body of knowledge. Indeed, only in C is there an instance in which one can be (all but) certain that *kynde wit* is a faculty and not a body of knowledge:

> Ac clergie cometh bote of syhte and kynde wit of sterres,
> As to be bore or bygete in such a constillacioun,
> That wit wexeth therof and oþer wordes bothe.

---

[12] At B XII 64ff. we are told that *kynde wit* proceeds from *quod vidimus*, 'what we have seen', whereas *clergie* comes from *quod scimus*, 'what we know', and is a *konnynge of hevene* (the 'of' can probably mean both 'from' and 'concerning'), plainly not earthbound in the way that *kynde wit* seems to be. See also B XII 128ff. and my discussion below.

[13] Moral teaching is enabled by what *kynde wit* witnesses; at B XII 236ff. we are told how 'men by old tyme' derived moral *ensamples* 'of briddes and of beestes'. At B XII 128ff. one of the sources of *kynde wit* is 'briddes and . . . beestes'.

[14] Pearsall (1978) on C Prologue 141, p. 37. For *kynde wit* as unillumined by divine revelation see B XII 105ff.; 126ff. I shall argue that *kynde wit* is redefined so as to give it this characteristic.

*Vultus huius seculi sunt subiecti vultibus celestibus.*
So grace is a gifte of god and kynde wit a chaunce
And clergie a connynge of kynde wittes techyng.

(C XIV 30–4)

Yet in the equivalent B passage *kynde wit* cannot possibly be a faculty:

Clergie and kynde wit cometh of sighte and techyng,
As the Book bereth witnesse to burnes that kan rede:
*Quod scimus loquimur, quod vidimus testamur.*
Of *quod scimus* cometh clergie, a konnynge of hevene,
And of *quod vidimus* cometh kynde wit, of sighte of diverse peple.

(B XII 64–7)

It is also to be noted that the distinction between the *kynde wit*s of these passages is not just between a faculty and what that faculty perceives. The establishment of the body of knowledge referred to in B is not totally dependent on the high intelligence of which C speaks, and it is clear that C's *kynde wit* contributes to *clergie* (which the following lines show to be theological knowledge as in B) rather than producing a body of knowledge distinct from it – *kynde wit* in B's understanding. This illustrates the flexibility of the term *kynde wit* in Langland's usage, in view of which I shall not attempt a single, all-embracing definition of *kynde wit*, but concentrate rather on what the term might mean at particular points.

It is also necessary to do justice to Langland's adjective *kynde*. Even if Langland's term could always be aligned with *scientia* or *vis cogitativa*, one must be clear that he saw fit to emphasise the *kynde*ness of the *wit* in question. I have already suggested that it is the naturalness of *kynde wit* which makes it such an important term for Langland, and I shall later be considering the possibility that its naturalness is bound up with the unsatis-factoriness Langland discovers in it.

Consideration of the meaning of *kynde wit* in what follows is worked into a review of what Langland takes to be the function of *kynde wit* and his view of its efficacy in the pursuit of salvation. Langland's estimate of *kynde wit* seems to me to change as the poem progresses: initially it appears in a highly positive light, being seen to contribute in various ways to the cause of Good – this is why Tolkien could gloss it '(natural) good sense' – but Ymaginatif makes *kynde wit* the subject of a scrutiny by no means flattering. Quite how Ymaginatif's *kynde wit* stands in relation to *kynde wit* earlier in the poem is a matter which requires some discussion, but it can be argued that after Ymaginatif's appraisal Langland is unable to look upon *kynde wit* again as sanguinely as he once had done; the hope he had invested in the term cannot be relocated there with full conviction. In the end, I think, Langland finds that *kynde wit* cannot be made the vehicle of his optimism about man's natural condition. I see Ymaginatif's intervention as pivotal in the fortunes of *kynde wit*, and this determines the broad lines of my treatment.

## Kynde Wit

*Kynde wit* is first mentioned in the following passage:

"*Reddite cesari,*" quaþ god, "þat *cesari* befall[iþ],
*Et que sunt dei deo* oþer ellis ȝe don ille."
For riȝtfulliche resoun shulde rewele ȝow alle,
And kynde wyt be wardeyn ȝoure welþe to kepe,
And tutour of ȝour tresour, & take it ȝow at nede;
For husbondrie & he holden togidires.

(A I 50–5)

One might seek to gloss *kynde wit* here 'common sense', or 'natural good sense', in accordance with Skeat and Tolkien, and suppose that we are being told that common sense recommends being sensible with money. But it is equally possible to understand *kynde wit* as a faculty or a body of knowledge which permits the perception of a moral law relating to not wasting and consuming only what one needs, to the practice of moderation, in fact. Such moderation is frequently in medieval literature the counsel of Nature,[15] and its practice may be considered an item in the natural law. That law, in its moral aspect, is orthodoxly understood to be revealed to man through his natural reason, and natural reason seems an appropriate gloss here.

The plausibility of this gloss and the proximity in which reason and nature stand in this passage raise the question of the relation *kynde wit* bears to reason. Several critics have thought the two identical or nearly so in *Piers Plowman*.[16] But one wonders why, in that case, Langland bothered to use two terms for the same thing. Those who identify the two terms tend to see Reason in *Piers Plowman* as a faculty, but very frequently Reason can be understood rather as a principle, as the Reasonable or the Right.[17] In some places it is impossible, I think, to take Reason as a faculty. In B XI, in the *Myddelerthe* scene, Will sees Reason *sewe* the beasts and fail to *sewe* man. But medieval thought supposes that men possess the faculty reason and that the animals lack it. Langland's point is that animals behave in accordance with the Right, whilst men (in virtue of their possession of the faculty reason with its power of moral choice) fail to do this.[18] *Kynde wit*'s separateness from Reason in *Piers Plowman* could be explained with reference to this

---

[15] See, for instance, the ending of Jean de Hautville's *Architrenius*, ed. P. G. Schmidt (München, 1974), where the hero of the poem is married to Moderantia by Natura.

[16] See, e.g., Dunning (1937), pp. 39–40 (endorsed by Kean (1964), p. 243, n. 2); Anna Baldwin, *The Theme of Government in Piers Plowman* (Cambridge, 1981), pp. 21–2. We might also observe that at B XII 104ff. *lettrure*, which stands in implicit contrast to *kynde wit*, leads to reason (Quirk (1953), p. 184 points this out).

[17] For this sense see the *Middle English Dictionary*, ed. H. Kurath, S. M. Kuhn, R. E. Lewis and J. Reidy, under resoun, 2.

[18] Priscilla Martin, *Piers Plowman: the Field and the Tower* (London, 1979), p. 95 and J. Norton-Smith, *William Langland* (London, 1980), pp. 113–14 both suggest that Langland is here endowing the animals with a rational faculty. Animals certainly have *kynde wit* (at least they do in C), but in them that does not have to be understood as reason; Quirk (1953) regards *kynde wit* in animals as the *vis aestimativa* which corresponds to the *vis cogitativa* in humans, but is not identical with it.

sense of Reason. And its alliance with Reason in this passage and elsewhere can be understood to indicate a basic capacity in man to recognise what is right. This would be entirely orthodox: the natural reason can perceive the natural law, and that law enshrines the moral precepts of the gospel.[19]

However we take *kynde wit* here, its association with Reason validates *kynde wit* and lends authority to its moral pronouncements. The high standing of *kynde wit* is evident too in its connection with *husbondrie*, a notion which is bound up with central Langlandian concerns. Piers enshrines this virtue, carefully providing for the physical needs of the community and running up against the *wastours*, the countering of whom exercises him so strenuously.[20] Even from this brief passage we can see that *kynde wit* stands for good living against forces powerfully disruptive of the well-ordered society.

*Kynde wit*'s partnership with *husbondrie* harmonises with its injunction that men should labour:

> Kynde wyt wolde þat iche wiȝt wrouȝte
> Oþer wiþ teching, oþer telling, or trauaillyng of hondis,
> Actif lif oþer contemplatif; crist wolde it alse.

(A VII 231–3)

Kynde wit is here made to urge a doctrine of enormous importance to Langland, one that lies at the heart of the vision of the good life projected on Piers' half-acre. And the insistence here on the natural accessibility of this doctrine – Langland refers to Christ only secondarily – seems to show that Langland wishes to suggest that at a fundamental level man is naturally guided towards virtuous living.

We might note two further things about this passage. Firstly, we can glimpse here in embryo human society, with its specialised forms of activity.

[19] So for Aquinas the first principles of natural law are 'scripta in ratione naturali' and are 'per se nota rationi humanae' (*Summa Theologica* I II q.100 a.3 and a.3 ad 1). Aquinas also states that the 'prima et communia praecepta' of the natural law are love of God and of neighbour (*Summa Theologica* I II q.100 a.3 ad 1). Gratian writes:

> Ius naturae est, quod in lege et euangelio continetur, quo quisque iubetur alii facere, quod sibi uult fieri, et prohibetur alii inferre, quod sibi nolit fieri.
> (*Decretum* Dist. I dictum ante c. 1)

In the 15th century *Dives and Pauper*, ed. P. H. Barnum, *EETS* 275, 280 (Oxford, 1976, 1980) Vol. I Part 2, p. 28 we are told that

> alle þe ten comandementis ben conteynyd in þe two preceptis of charite and þe two preceptis of charite ben conteynyd & knyt in þis on precept of kende: Quod tibi non vis fieri alteri ne facias, . . . . And so, . . . . al þe lawe is conteynyd in þis on precept of kende: þat þu wil nout ben don to þe, do þu it to non oþir;

Brian Tierney, 'Natura, id est Deus, A Case of Juristic Pantheism?', *Journal of the History of Ideas*, 24 (1963), 307–22 provides a useful review of medieval and particularly juristic thought on the Law of Nature.
[20] See A VII 107ff.

Langland will develop further *kynde wit*'s role as instituter and organiser of human society, with its separate estates in the B Prologue, and I shall suggest that this involvement in societal forms may be bound up with *kynde wit*'s fall from grace. Secondly, *kynde wit* accepts the contemplative life as one kind of labour.[21] This, I think, makes it very difficult to hold that *kynde wit* is only *scientia* or that it is limited to *temporalia*. It also seems to rule out the idea that *kynde wit* is tied to the physical *bonum*, though, in fact, I think it might be argued that its concern with that kind of good is excessive. *Kynde wit* evidently has spiritual concerns, and it seems most implausible to suggest that those concerns only arise out of its primary commitment to physical well-being.[22]

It is also highly unlikely that Langland would associate *kynde wit* as insistently as he does with Conscience, were *kynde wit*'s essential concern with *temporalia* or the physical *bonum*. It is true that in C Langland speaks of men and animals possessing 'a cantel of kynde wyt here kynde to saue' (XIV 163), but this knowledge of how the *kynde* is to be preserved, need not exhaust the capacities of human *kynde wit*. Our understanding of the term has to be wide enough to embrace both this aspect of *kynde wit* and its moral competence. Its moral status appears all the greater when we realise that it is often not merely an associate of Conscience, but in a sense the senior partner in the alliance.[23] Such seniority is apparent when *kynde wit* is presented, as it frequently is, as Conscience's teacher, but it is also perhaps detectable in the following passage. Conscience has been looking forward,

[21] A's idea of the contemplative life seems rather an unusual one, concentrating as it apparently does on teaching. Kane (1960) on A VII 232, p. 449 wonders about the correctness of *hondis* and suspects *preyeres* may have been the original reading. *Teching* could then refer to the mixed life rather than the contemplative. All B manuscripts have 'Or in dikynge or in deluynge or travaillynge in preieres', or something very close to this. This Schmidt emends to 'Or in [te]chynge or in [tell]ynge or travaillynge in preieres' (B VI 248), and the reading is similar in Kane and Donaldson's text (George Kane and E. Talbot Donaldson, *Piers Plowman: The B Version* (London, 1975)). As the manuscripts stand, however, B differs widely from A and offers a more orthodox view of the contemplative life. See M. R. Godden, 'Plowmen and Hermits in Langland's *Piers Plowman*', *RES*, n.s. 35 (1984), 129–63 (p. 135).

[22] Even in the A text, where the contemplative life is apparently understood as a life of teaching, it is highly unlikely that the idea of contemplation would have been invoked if what was in mind was instruction concerning the physical and the temporal. Wishing to see Kynde Wit as tied to the physical, Harwood (1976) has to resort to the notion of figure when dealing with Conscience's being taught by Kynde Wit, with Anima's discourse in B XV, with Kynde Wit's involvement in the building of the ditch Holiness in B XIX and with Kynde Wit's showing Piers the way to Truth (B V 539). Harwood supposes that Piers' conception of God and of the relationship between God and himself are vitiated because Piers uses (metaphorically) the idea of *kynde wit*. Harwood's questioning of Piers' apparent trust in the competence of Kynde Wit and his reading of the tearing of the pardon as an indictment of Kynde Wit seem appropriate, but his inadmissible restriction of the sense of the term leads him, in my view, to formulate his worries in the wrong way.

[23] However, M. C. Schroeder, 'The Character of Conscience in *Piers Plowman*', *Studies in Philology*, 67 (1970), 13–30 sees its association with Kynde Wit as a mark of Conscience's limitation (p. 21).

9

rather apocalyptically, to the demise of Mede. *Kynde wit* takes pride of place when Conscience rounds off his speech and the Passus by telling us

> Ac kynde wit shal come ʒet, & consience togidere,
> And make of lawe a labourer, such loue shal arise.

> (A III 275–6)

Langland's order perhaps stresses again the naturalness to man of the good life: it is simply (though this is not, in fact, so simple) a matter of following what our *kynde wit* dictates.

It should be remarked that *kynde wit* is here once more concerned with the structures of society and that labour is crucial in society as he sees it. But, more than this, *kynde wit* is at least intimately involved in, if not actually responsible for, the institution of an ideal society in which love flourishes. Kynde Wit's connections have already authenticated him as a considerable force for good, but this close association with Love, the supreme Christian virtue, revealed as it is at the culmination of an ecstatic vision of future blessedness, seems finally to disallow the relatively disparaging definitions offered by Jones, Robertson and Huppé and Harwood, and to invest Kynde Wit with tremendous moral power.

The context of the last quoted passage also liberates the possibilities of word-play always latent in the term *kynde*. Kynde Wit and Conscience are to come into a world in which

> Mede of mysdoeris makiþ hem so riche
> Þat lawe is lord waxen & leute is pore,
> Vnkyndenesse is comaundour, & kyndenesse is banisshit.

> (A III 272–4)

The *kynde wit* of the next line then appears as something attuned to the demands of *kyndenesse*. Indeed the term itself seems to claim as much, since the adjective inevitably tends to take on the colour of the *kynde* terms which immediately precede it. So *kynde wit* is the *wit* that pursues *kyndenesse*. That term, as we shall see later,[24] involves us in problems of its own, but it can probably here be taken both as 'naturally appropriate behaviour' and as 'kindness' in the modern sense. Certainly no difficulty arises in attaching the idea of benevolence to *kynde wit* since, as we have seen, *kynde wit* announces principles central in Langland's understanding of the good life and is closely linked with Love.

Kynde Wit's priority to Conscience is clearly apparent a little earlier in Conscience's speech:

> [I] consience knowe þis, for kynde [w]it me tauʒte,
> Þat resoun shal regne & reumes gouerne,
> And riʒt as agag hadde happe shal somme:

---

[24] See Chapter 4.

Samuel shal slen hym, & saul shal be blamid,
And dauid shal be dyademid & daunten hem alle,
And o cristene king kepe vs ichone.
Shal no more mede be maister on erþe,
But loue & louȝnesse & leaute togideris;

(A III 260–7)

Here, as the recurrent connection of Kynde Wit with society appears again, Kynde Wit is represented not as urging a course of action, but as predicting events, though in view of what is to follow shortly we might well suppose that Kynde Wit, like Conscience, enthusiastically endorses the state of affairs he foresees. The events predicted certainly suggest the appropriateness of a life lived in accordance with the principles of Reason and Love, *louȝnesse* and *leaute*; since these seem to be the ultimate reality, their side that which will eventually overcome, one would be ill-advised to throw in one's lot with the side opposing them.

Kynde Wit here seems to be drawing on a specifically Christian eschatological tradition.[25] One might, straining rather hard, suppose that the apocalyptic utopia of which Conscience speaks could, in Langland's view, be deduced from a vision of God available to Christians and non-Christians alike, and hence find 'natural reason (unillumined by divine revelation)' an appropriate gloss for Kynde Wit: the Christian Conscience would then be filling out the Christian details on the basis of fundamental truths available to all men.[26] But, whatever the plausibility of this picture, it is derived from an unnatural reading of the text. It is easier to take it that Kynde Wit is in possession of all the details of the apocalyptic picture and that, consequently, he *is* illuminated by the Christian revelation. Langland is not concerned at this stage to examine what can be done without benefit of revelation, but to suggest that certain crucial truths and moral principles are readily available to every Christian.

Langland's initial concern in *Piers Plowman* is with Christian souls and Christian societies, and what his use of *kynde wit* in the early stages of the poem seems to imply is that such souls and such societies are in touch at a basic level with the good. Regarding the association between Kynde Wit and Conscience, it may be said that man's moral faculty, that within him which attempts to choose the good, is guided by awarenesses of moral rules or facts with a moral bearing laid up in a faculty or a body of knowledge so basic to man that it can be called *kynde*. This adjective perhaps points to Langland's

---

[25] On this tradition see Norman Cohn, *The Pursuit of the Millenium* (London, 1970), pp. 19–36.

[26] Virgil's Sixth *Eclogue* would offer an example of pagan 'millenarianism'. Thus we might just possibly have here a Christian unfolding of an understanding of the universe, not essentially Christian, as controlled by a benign or just power (we might go to the *Consolation of Philosophy*, where Boethius prohibits himself obviously Christian resources, or to the *Somnium Scipionis* for such understandings).

frustration at the perversity of man in remaining sinful: man knows *perfectly well* what he has to do. And this simple following of the dictates of a conscience guided by *kynde wit*, would issue, so Kynde Wit's eschatological role suggests, in a world of honest labour in which love reigned paramount.

This view of *kynde wit* may seem rather exorbitant. Perhaps all we have to do is to follow the dictates of what we all as Christians know, but to state the matter thus is to omit reference to the crucial role that has to be played by grace if our pursuit of what we know is to be done is to end in success. Later in the poem *kynde wit* is aligned against *clergie* and grace and found incapable of bringing man to salvation. Langland there appears to be modifying an earlier conviction regarding the significance and efficacy of *kynde wit* in the quest for salvation. It may be that a realisation that Conscience had claimed too much for *kynde wit* at the end of Passus A III led the poet to substitute *kynde love* for *kynde wit* in the equivalent B and C passages (see B III 299; C III 451). Langland often returns us to the fundamental structures of man's existence as a starting point for an elaboration of the good life, as if he believes, or would like to believe, that at man's beginnings, as it were, all is well.[27] It may be for this reason that the hero of the poem is one intimately tied to the very basic purpose of food-production (furthermore, Piers is, or comes to be seen as,[28] the type of the *kynde wit*ted man). But Langland experiences also the failure of his elaborations of the good life based on the fundamental configurations of man, and the development of the poem as a whole can be seen as involving a movement away from a conviction that salvation is essentially vested in the capacities of man, to an awareness that it has to be achieved for him through the action of the divine.[29] It might be objected that in the case presently under consideration, one item of man's natural equipment is substituted for another, but I suspect

---

[27] Such returns occur with the description of the grounds of society in the B Prologue and with the institution of Piers' society in B VI. The society of Grace in B XIX can be seen as a new beginning for mankind. A different kind of return to the fundamental structures of man's existence occurs when Wit describes the Castle of *Caro* in Passus B IX; here again, Langland seems to want to believe that at root all is well with man. The first three idealisations display themselves as just that rather quickly, and I shall suggest in Chapter 3 that Langland comes to find his Castle of *Caro* allegory unrealistic.

[28] I offer this rider because in A Piers does not actually claim that *kynde wit* guides him to Truth, speaking only of wit. I doubt, however, that he means anything other than *kynde wit*. See note 1.

[29] The poem devolves upon the Incarnation, in which, perhaps, man's need for God, if he is to be saved, is made most dramatically apparent. At the end of the poem it appears that the presence of Grace is necessary if human efforts to keep viable a system of salvation are not to end in collapse. Conscience, a human faculty, is still at least reaching out for the assistance of the divine, but in the last line of the poem he is shown calling out for Grace, and the incapacity of man unaided by God is thereby emphatically acknowledged. See Helen Barr, 'The Use of Latin Quotations in *Piers Plowman* with special reference to Passus XVIII of the 'B' Text', *N&Q*, n.s. 33 (1986), 440–8.

that the *kynde* in *kynde love* does not mean 'innate' or 'natural', but rather 'proper' or 'authentic'.[30] However, even if *kynde love* were to be taken as in some way innate or otherwise natural to us, its activity is clearly muted in the normal sinful course of things in a way that of *kynde wit* is not, so that its coming in triumph requires much more obviously the grace of the divine.

Whatever the reasons behind the change from *kynde wit* to *kynde love*, the status of *kynde wit* in the later versions of the poem is, though not initially, reduced. Before we turn to these versions, however, the treatment of Kynde Wit in A XII demands attention. The Passus is, of course, only dubiously Langlandian, so that what it has to say about Kynde Wit may be of no relevance to what Langland thinks of the concept.[31] Nevertheless, what it has to say is of great interest.

At the end of Passus A XI, frustrated by the discourse of Clergie, which he feels has brought him no nearer a knowledge of *dowel*, Will breaks into a diatribe in which he claims learning is of no use in the quest for salvation and that the simple are more easily saved than are *clerkis*. In response to this, at the beginning of Passus A XII Clergie says that he would give Will an answer to his questions if he knew that he would act in accordance with the teaching. At this point Scripture intervenes:

> Skornfully þ[o] scripture she[t] vp h[ere] browes,
> And on clergie crieþ on crist*es* holy name
> That he shewe me hit ne sholde but ȝif [I schriue*n*] were
> Of þe kynde cardinal wit, and cristned in a font,
>
> (A XII 12–15)

'þe kynde cardinal wit'[32] seems to be Kynde Wit, for in response to Scripture's speech Will asks her to direct him to 'Kynde [wit] hure co*n*fessou*r*' and her cousin (A XII 41). Scripture's response shows her approval of Will's request:

> Þat lady þa*n* low and lauȝthe me in her*e* armes
> And sayde, 'my cosyn kynde wit knowe*n* is wel wide,
> And his loggyng is wit*h* lyf þat lord is of erþe,
> And ȝif þou desyre wit*h* hym for to abyde
> I shal þe wisse [wynlyche] wher*e* þat he dwelleth'.
>
> (A XII 42–6)

---

[30] For this meaning see MED under kind(e adj. 2 and my discussion in the next chapter. One might not wish to disallow the sense 'natural' entirely, since it is no doubt true that the capacity to love is innate in us in virtue of the remnants of our unfallen nature. But I suppose Langland is primarily thinking of a fulfilment of the nature of love such that it is true or proper (as in its nature it *really* is). See Chapter 2, note 8.

[31] The manuscript evidence suggests that the A version at one stage concluded at the end of Passus XI. It is still possible, however, that Langland wrote at least some of Passus XII as an abortive continuation.

[32] In this phrase there is perhaps some uncertainty over the meaning of *kynde* and what it qualifies.

To guide Will Scripture summons

> a clerioun þat
> Hyȝt *omnia probate*, a pore þing wi*th*alle;
> 'Þou shalt wende wi*th* wil,' q*uo*d she, 'whiles þat hi*m* lykyþ,
> Til ȝe come to þe burg[h] *quod bonum est tenete.*
> Ken hi*m* to my cosenes hous þat kinde wit hyȝth.
> Sey I sente hi*m* þis segge, and þat he shewe hy*m* dowel.'

(A XII 49–54)

Thus Kynde Wit appears as a crucial figure on the road to salvation. Acquisition of *kynde wit* seems to be necessary before the lessons of Clergie can be properly appreciated. That acquisition requires that one 'prove everything', which activity is a prelude, apparently, to holding fast to what is good.[33] This holding fast to what is good is apparently a condition for acquiring *kynde wit*, and that acquisition will enable one to know what *dowel* is. There seems to be some duplication in the allegory here, since to hold fast to what is good surely requires a knowledge of *dowel*, so that Kynde Wit's subsequent showing of *dowel* appears to be redundant. But however we interpret the allegorical action here, it is very evident that Kynde Wit is a considerable force for good. Indeed, by the end of the sequence of passages quoted, Kynde Wit seems to have gone beyond being the preliminary to further advancement and to have become, effectively, the final goal of Will's search: the possession of *kynde wit* seems to involve the knowledge and practice of the good. What has not been apparent in previous references to Kynde Wit is the necessity for a journey to find him. Now the arduous task of proving everything lies between the possession of *kynde wit* and its seeker. But the *kynde* of Kynde Wit may still point to the accessibility of what now appears as its vital wisdom. Will's journey involves him in such ordinary experiences as hunger and disease, and Kynde Wit's being known 'wel wide' and his dwelling with 'lyf þat lord is of erþe' perhaps indicate that he is to be acquired through the process of exposure to the ordinary vicissitudes of living rather than in any more arcane way.

---

[33] The *omnia probate* text occurs several times in *Piers Plowman*. Besides this passage see B III 336ff. and C XX 234a. The ease with which it springs to Langland's mind is suggested by the use Conscience makes of it in dealing with Lady Mede (B III 336ff.). Its appearance is by no means strictly necessary, since it only provides a parallel with which to illustrate the suspect nature of Mede's citation of another text. This is, perhaps, a small indication of how the idea of experience commanded Langland's interest.

One might be tempted, on the evidence of A XII, to see experience as a necessary condition for *kynde wit*, even where this is not made explicit. But Piers has been a follower of Truth for forty winters (B V 542), and yet was 'kenned . . . to his place' and made to promise to serve him by Conscience and Kynde Wit (B V 539–40), which perhaps suggests that Kynde Wit in this very important instance does not involve extensive experience. It is certainly not obvious that Langland always wishes us to understand Kynde Wit as achieved through the suffering experience involves, which is what may well be suggested in A XII and B XX.

I shall be suggesting later that the experience of passing through life towards death, an experience he sets under the auspices of Kynde, is seen by Langland in B and C as a powerful stimulus to good. It may be that here in Passus A XII we have an early attempt upon this territory. At the end of B and C forces apparently hostile to him operate on Will in such a way as to encourage him to enter Unity and to love. In Passsus A XII Fever who is a servant of Death shows himself concerned for Will's moral welfare. Fever is on an errand from Death to Life, an errand that will lead to Life's death. Will, perhaps because he has been told that Kynde Wit dwells with Life, but possibly rather because he can no longer endure the suffering the meeting with Fever has brought, asks to go with Fever. Fever replies:

> 'Nay, wil,' . . . . 'wend þou no ferther,
> But lyue as þis lyf is ordeyned for the.
> Þ[ou] tomblest wiþ a trepget ȝif þou my tras folwe,
> And mannes merþe w[or]þ no mor þan he deseruyþ here
> Whil his lyf and his lykhame lesten togedere.
> And þerfore do after dowel whil þi dayes duren,
> Þat þi play be plentevous in paradys with aungelys.
> Þou shalt be lauȝth into lyȝth with loking of an eye
> So þat þou werke þe word þat holy wryt techeþ,
> And be prest to preyeres and profitable werkes.'
>
> (A XII 89–98)

The threat of death makes one realise how urgent the task is of earning one's eternal reward. Proving everything is plainly thrusting Will towards *dowel*; perhaps we are to suppose that at the end of A he has acquired Kynde Wit – certainly he has heard the wisdom derived from natural experience.

I have suggested that Kynde Wit is seen in A as a powerful force in the establishment of society as it should be. Early in B and C this function of *kynde wit* is given explicit treatment. Kynde Wit is a prominent figure in the institution of society in the B and C Prologues:

> Thanne kam ther a Kyng: Knyghthod hym ladde;
> Might of the communes made hym to regne.
> And thanne cam Kynde Wit and clerkes he made,
> For to counseillen the Kyng and the Commune save.
> The Kyng and Knyghthod and Clergie bothe
> Casten that the Commune sholde hem [communes] fynde.
> The Commune contreved of Kynde Wit craftes,
> And for profit of al the peple plowmen ordeyned
> To tilie and to travaille as trewe lif asketh.
> The Kyng and the Commune and Kynde Wit the thridde
> Shopen lawe and leaute – ech lif to knowe his owene.
>
> (B Prol. 112–22)

The C version of this passage shows several changes, but in respect of Kynde

Wit, at least, these changes produce a clarification rather than a radical alteration of the original picture:[34]

> Thenne cam ther a kyng, knyghthede hym ladde,
> Myght of tho men made hym to regne.
> And thenne cam Kynde Wytt and clerkus he made
> And Conscience and Kynde Wit and knyghthed togedres
> Caste þat þe comunes sholde here comunes fynde.
> Kynde Wytt and þe comune contreued alle craftes
> And for most profitable a plogh gonne þei make,
> With lele labour to lyue while lif on londe lasteth.

(C Prol. 139–46)

And after this passage in C Kynde Wit has the words given to a lunatic in B:

> Thenne Kynde Witt to þe kynge and to þe comune saide,
> 'Crist kepe þe, kynge, and thy kyneriche
> And leue the lede so þy londe þat Lewte þe louye
> And for thy rightful ruylynge be rewardid in heuene.'

(C Prol. 147–50)

Kynde Wit here is responsible for several things vital to the maintenance of an ordered and right-living society. In the first place, he makes *clerkes*. One can take this in different ways; it may be that Kynde Wit dictates that there should be learned men who can advise the King and attend to the welfare of the Commune. Or it may be that Kynde Wit should here be understood as a body of knowledge mastery of which makes men *clerkes*. Thirdly, Kynde Wit might be understood as native intelligence (in the sense of high intelligence) the possession of which permits men to become *clerkes*.[35] However we understand the relation between Clergie and Kynde Wit, there is no suggestion of the later opposition between them, which has Clergie in possession of a wisdom unreachable by Kynde Wit, and which operates so as to undermine *kynde wit*'s authority and its status. Here, the authority and status of Kynde Wit are evident as he stands ultimately responsible for the fundamental arrangements of a society committed to *lawe* and *leaute*.[36]

Very prominent among the concerns of the society Langland presents (which is presumably an image of society in general) is the production of food, and Kynde Wit's provision of ploughmen to supply that need and his contriving of other crafts demonstrates his concern with the physical *bonum*. It is, however, unlikely that Langland means us to regard the whole social structure as a mechanism for ensuring survival, its laws and its *leaute* only

---

[34] For a consideration of the import of the changes here in relation to Langland's views on government see E. T. Donaldson, *Piers Plowman: The C-text and its Poet* (New Haven, 1949), pp. 85ff. and Baldwin (1981), pp. 15f.

[35] This seems to be the meaning of *kynde wit* at C XIV 30–4. There, rather as in the B Prologue passage, Clergie is described as 'a connynge of kynde wittes techyng'. See Janet Coleman, *Piers Plowman and the Moderni* (Roma, 1981), p. 59.

[36] The responsibility is very apparent in the C version of the passage, but is also clearly implicit in B.

instruments towards that end. Certainly Langland sees the mutual physical 'profit' of its members as one of the ends of society, but medieval thinking on the state regarded it as a remedy for the sin that had been introduced onto the human scene by the Fall:[37] the state has, in fact, a moral function. In Langland's treatment of the institution of the state *leaute* is an end rather than a means, whilst the goodness of *trewe lif* and *lele labour* does not lie solely in the contribution they make to the physical well-being of the community. For Langland morality does not serve production; rather, the validity of the life of honest labour lies in its compatibility with a morality based in the non-material. But though it is not possible to see society as instituted solely in order that food shall be produced and men survive, it is possible to argue that society's concern with the preservation of the body compromises it: Langland, I think, does not always believe in the validity of the life of honest labour.[38]

Kynde Wit's responsibility for the social structure may extend to the King himself. Langland is perhaps pointing to the naturalness of monarchical authority: the idea could be paralleled in legal writing.[39] But it may be significant that Kynde Wit takes the stage only after the appearance of King and knights. Monarchy is not viewed as the only acceptable (and therefore natural) form of state in medieval legal theory, and Langland may wish to avoid giving the impression that it is.[40] However this may be, Langland does seem to be claiming that man has a natural capacity to create the state's coercive apparatus of laws and the estates structure which act as counters to the disorder and anarchy that would be inevitable in the fallen world if 'ech lif' did not 'knowe his owene'.[41]

[37] See Dunning (1937) pp. 88ff.; A. P. D'Entrèves, *The Medieval Contribution to Political Thought* (Oxford, 1939), pp. 32ff. For extended discussion of medieval thought on the function of the state see R. W. and A. J. Carlyle, *A History of Medieval Political Theory in the West* (Edinburgh/London, 1903–36), e.g., I 164–74; III 106–14. Piers' social contract with the Knight gives the Knight a function related to the production of food (B VI 24ff.) but Piers also requires the Knight to operate in accordance with Truth and *mekenesse* (B VI 37ff.)

[38] See Godden (1984).

[39] See Sir John Fortescue, *De Natura Legis Nature*, I xviii, cited by Myra Stokes, *Justice and Mercy in Piers Plowman* (London/Canberra, 1984), p. 69.

[40] For writers who saw the republic as an acceptable configuration of the state see Otto Gierke, *Political Theories of the Middle Age*, trans. F. W. Maitland (Cambridge, 1900), pp. 32f. with notes 112–18 (pp. 140–1).

[41] Donaldson (1949), p. 89, takes the phrase 'ech lif to knowe his owene' as having reference to the differing positions and duties of members of society. Kean (1964), on the other hand, argues (p. 243) that in view of the immediate context of concern about how temporal goods are to be provided, we should understand the phrase to refer to the property of individuals. John of Salisbury's *Policraticus* speaks of how:

Philosophi gentium, iustitiam, quae politica dicitur, praeceptis et moribus informantes, . . . unumquemque suis rebus et studiis uoluerunt esse contentum, urbanis et suburbanis, colonis quoque uel rusticis sua singulis loca et studia praescribentes.

(I cap. 3)

See also Stokes (1984), p. 69, and her citation from the *Policraticus* in note 21 (p. 96).

As a parallel to the role Langland gives Kynde Wit here, P. M. Kean adduces Aquinas' conception of human law as proceeding from natural reason (which seems an appropriate gloss for Kynde Wit here).[42] For Aquinas, the first principles of the natural law are written in man's natural reason,[43] and whilst what we witness in Langland's scene is the promulgation of positive law, the crucial role played by Kynde Wit seems to indicate that that positive law will be, as it has to be to possess legitimacy, in line with the law of nature. Medieval thinking on natural law sees it as embodying the essential precepts both of the Old Law and the Gospel, so that the laws of Langland's society will be consonant with what Aquinas calls the *prima et communia precepta* of the natural law, love of God and of neighbour.[44]

Central to Langland's conception of what *kynde wit* can achieve in the sphere of society is its promotion of *leaute*. This term has been understood variously by different critics. Donaldson saw it as strict adherence to the letter of the law.[45] Were this the case, the way would be open to understanding the society of Kynde Wit as one of 'strict commutative and distributive justice'[46] in which mercy and love have no place. Yet such an understanding would not seem congruous with Kynde Wit's connection with a natural law that enjoins love, and which is frequently understood to require that one does to others as one would wish to be done by oneself. An angel offers the King advice reminiscent of this encapsulation of the natural law: '*Qualia vis metere, talia grana sere*' (B Prol. 136e), and it may be that the angel's speech does not correct Kynde Wit's institution, as has been suggested, but rather draws attention to something implicit in the founding of a society on *kynde wit*.[47] In the C text Kynde Wit invokes Christ in recommending that the King should rule rightfully so as to be loved by

---

[42] Kean (1964), p. 243.

[43] See note 19. For the need for positive law to be consonant with natural law see Carlyle (1903–36), II 78ff., 105–8; Stokes (1984), p. 53.

[44] See note 19.

[45] Donaldson (1949), p. 66.

[46] This is Coleman's view of the society under *kynde wit* (Coleman (1981), pp. 58ff.). Coleman does not, however, see *leaute* as strict adherence to the letter of the law. See below in the text and next note.

[47] Coleman (1981), pp. 62–3, makes the suggestion. But her discussion of this part of the poem seems to me unsatisfactory; for instance, for her the natural law society in B is one of strict justice, while *leaute* is 'a loyalty born of love rather than of strict commutative justice' (p. 62); yet *leaute* is something which Kynde Wit sponsors, as we have seen. Again, Coleman explains the transference of the lunatic's speech to Kynde Wit in C as a change 'in favour of man's *natural* powers to know that the *lex christi* is to be the righteous rule of law' (p. 64), yet the society Kynde Wit produces in C seems no more informed by the law of the Gospel than does that society in B. In fact, Kynde Wit's associations with love, which we have already examined, make it unlikely that a society he produced would be loveless. Willi Erzgräber, *William Langlands 'Piers Plowman' (Eine Interpretation des C-Textes)* (Heidelberg, 1957), p. 49, finds that Kynde Wit promotes a strict justice which has to be modified by the mercy Conscience counsels. He, though, is considering the C text. Stokes (1984), pp. 70–1, links *Qualia vis metere. . . .*' with 'do as you would be done by'.

Lewte. It seems unlikely that Christ would be called upon to *kepe* a King who ruled by strict justice alone. Furthermore, the angel's speech in C is given to Conscience whose association with Kynde Wit we have noted above. Would we expect Conscience to be at odds with Kynde Wit over the question of justice and mercy?

P. M. Kean, who in marking *leaute*'s connection with law and love demonstrated the importance of the term for Langland, has suggested that *leaute* means justice, where this is understood as complete virtue in relation to our neighbour,[48] and this would certainly fit with one's sense that a virtue Kynde Wit promulgates as a foundation for society must be capable of embracing love. It would also again accord Kynde Wit the high moral status it frequently has in Langland, rather more effectively than would Donaldson's suggestion. But both these requirements would be met by other definitions, such as Pearsall's and Coleman's. Coleman interprets *leaute* here as 'loyalty born of love rather than of strict commutative justice'[49] whilst Pearsall sees *leaute* as 'a loving recognition of the mutuality of obligation between man and man, or between a king and his subjects' and finds Piers and Christ represent the idea later in the poem.[50] Pearsall also points to the importance of Lewte as a recurrent personification: however precisely the concept is to be interpreted, it is clear that in it Kynde Wit sponsors a very significant virtue.

Kynde Wit, then, lies at the base of several aspects of society, its pursuit of food, its division into estates, its political system and its legal and moral framework. But why does Langland look back to the fundamental structures of society? The *aims* of society could be articulated without any reference to Kynde Wit. Langland may be wanting to validate the social structure by the reference to Kynde Wit, which shows it to be in accord with reason. But one might ask why Langland did not in this case have recourse to the figure Reason, whom he employs in the Mede episode to vindicate certain social arrangements. It may be that he wishes to stress the *kynde*ness of the good society, to make the point that it is within man's reach, at least to the extent that the principles of such a society are knoweable through *kynde wit*. Whether these principles will be followed is another matter: the optimism of Langland's projection is immediately qualified when he registers through the speech of the lunatic (Kynde Wit in C) that the King may not rule rightfully so as to be loved by Lewte. In general, the good behaviour of individuals cannot be guaranteed by the apparatus of the state. In the end, the good life is a matter of personal morality. But the claim for the *kynde* made here is a high one – and the claim is at least implicit, whatever the primary reason for Langland's deployment of Kynde Wit at this point: in some sense man has it

---

[48] Kean (1964), p. 256.
[49] Coleman (1981), p. 62.
[50] Pearsall (1978) on C Prologue 149, p. 37.

naturally within his grasp to impose a proper order on the chaotic field of folk.

Langland does not rest his case for *kynde wit* here. He ascribes it a role just in that area of personal morality which the laws of the state, however well administered, only touch superficially. Piers is taught the way to Truth by Conscience and Kynde Wit. But before we turn to Piers, we should follow the course of things in the state in the Mede episode. Here Langland sets his King a knotty problem in statesmanship. After considerable difficulty, Conscience, with the help of Reason manages to get the King to see that Lady Mede is unacceptable. At the moment of triumph, when Reason's arguments have swayed the King, Kynde Wit is reintroduced. Reason's rejection of Mede is bound up with an insistence on appropriate reward for good and evil expressed in his *nullum malum inpunitum, nullum bonum irremuneratum* conceit (B IV 143–4). The concern Kynde Wit has already shown for law suggests that he will find himself in agreement with Reason over the principle of reward according to desert and the rejection of Mede which it implies. Conscience in A had given Kynde Wit pride of place in the society of love which he opposed to the rule of Mede, and now Kynde Wit in person does something to substantiate Conscience's view of him. Furthermore Reason predicts that if the King follows his advice

> Lawe shal ben a laborer and lede afeld donge
> And Love shal lede thi lond as the leef liketh.
>
> (B IV 147–8)

These are precisely the conditions associated with the coming of Kynde Wit in A, so it is hardly surprising that he endorses Reason's views here in B:

> Alle rightfulle recorded that Reson truthe tolde.
> [Kynde] Wit acorded therwith and comendede hise wordes,
> And the mooste peple in the halle and manye of the grete,
> And leten Mekenesse a maister and Mede a mansed sherewe.
>
> (B IV 157–60)

C states Kynde Wit's agreement with Reason rather differently, implying that he has been instrumental in bringing about Reason's confutation of Mede:

> Ac al ryhtful recordede þat Resoun treuthe sayde
> And Kynde Wit and Consience corteysliche thonkede;
>
> (C IV 151–2)

C perhaps implies that the combination of Kynde Wit and Conscience has brought into being the right (Reasonable) decision regarding Mede, but it is evident both in B and C that Kynde Wit at least knows what is right. Why, though, does Langland reintroduce the concept of *kynde wit* at this stage? It may be that, as in the Prologue, he wishes us to see that the good society is within the grasp of man through his *kynde* endowment. This time we might feel that the claim has more substance. The good society Kynde Wit established in the Prologue existed at rather an abstract level, and its realisation in the actual world was problematic, as the Prologue itself acknowledged. The introduction of Kynde Wit into the Mede episode should perhaps take us back to the society of the Prologue and lead us to recognise the competence of a society based on Kynde Wit to cope with a difficult concrete social problem: Mede's kind of corruption can be dealt with, at least up to a point, in the Kynde Wit society – always supposing, of course, that the King is prepared to listen to the counsels of Reason and Conscience (counsels in harmony with the views of Kynde Wit). The society of the Prologue has now been tried in the fire and found capable of triumphing in the face of subtle and powerful opposition.

We might, I think, say that the Mede episode provides vindication for Langland's positive view of the *kynde* as this functions at the level of society. The promise of the society of the Prologue seems to have been fulfilled. And yet for all this, the success of Kynde Wit, Conscience and Reason in society at large does not guarantee the goodness of the individuals who comprise that society, and without that individual virtue the right functioning of state mechanisms is jeopardised: Mede's defeat is not absolute, indeed remains somewhat theoretical, as long as there are *sisours*, summoners and sheriff's clerks prepared to serve her still (see B IV 167–70). What is required, as the progress of the poem indicates with the move into the Repentance sequence, is virtue at the personal level.

We have already seen Kynde Wit instructing the individual as to how to spend his money; *kynde wit* inculcates within the individual the important principle of *mesure*. Again, Kynde Wit's beneficial effect on society in Conscience's prophecy (A III 260ff.; B III 284ff.; C III 436ff.) seems likely to be the result of its efficacy at the personal level in stimulating love. But the most powerful presentation of Kynde Wit's effectiveness in the moral life of the individual is in the figure of Piers as he first appears in the poem. Kynde Wit lay behind the demand for *trewe lif* made of the ploughmen in the Prologue: we now see Kynde Wit helping a ploughman to live that *trewe lif*. The first words Piers utters in the poem stress the importance of Kynde Wit in his service of Truth:

> I knowe hym [Truth] as kyndely as clerc doth hise bokes.
> Conscience and Kynde Wit kenned me to his place
> And diden me suren hym si[ththen] to serven hym for evere,
> Bothe to sowe and to sette while I swynke myghte.
>
> (B V 538–41)

Piers will later describe the way to Truth, and we may, I think, take it that that description enshrines what he has been taught by Kynde Wit and Conscience. Piers stands as the representative of the good life, and what is said so prominently of Kynde Wit and Conscience seems to make them the essential instruments in the pursuit of salvation. This high claim requires that we should seek to establish as nearly as possible what at this point Kynde Wit is. This is the first time in the poem in which the recurrent opposition between *kynde wit* and *clergie* appears. Later in the poem these terms are going to be used to cover the opposition between what is naturally known and what is revealed, but it is not clear that Kynde Wit here is to be taken as natural reason unaided by divine revelation. The way to Truth Piers describes embodies the Decalogue, which is orthodoxly held to be encapsulated in the natural law known to man's unaided natural reason.[51] But Piers' description of the route also includes several specifically Christian items. The walls of the *manoir* of Mercy are

> kerneled with Cristendom that kynde to save,
> Botrased with "Bileef-so-or-thow-beest-noght-saved."

(B V 588–9)

A little later we hear that

> The brugge is of "Bidde-wel-the-bet-may-thow-spede;"
> Ech piler is of penaunce, of preieres to seyntes;
> Of almesdedes are the hokes that the gates hangen on.

(B V 592–4)

Piers also requires the performance of penance enjoined by a priest and contrition (V 598–9), he tells of the importance of the seven virtues (V 618ff.) and he knows too of the roles played by Grace and Mary in salvation (V 595, 605; 603a). One might argue those items not actually directives need not form part of Conscience and Kynde Wit's teaching of the way to Truth: moral instruction need make no mention of Mary and Grace, and Piers' knowledge of them may be supposed to come from some other source. But this supposition seems rather gratuitous, the more so if we allow some Christian elements to be taught by Kynde Wit.

The truth is that Langland is not (yet) concerned with pagans, in relation to whom a consideration of the capacities of unillumined natural reason might be to the point. And, in fact, the claim that would be made for this pagan natural reason would almost certainly be excessive – what Langland says later in the poem about *kynde wit* when it does seem to mean unillumined natural reason suggests very strongly that he would not think that, so understood, it could lead to Truth.[52] But Piers is quite plainly a Christian within a Christian society. The contrast between Kynde Wit and Clergie to which Piers' words point is surely not one between the unillumined pagan and the Christian in possession of revelation but between the ordinary

[51] See note 19.
[52] See discussion below.

unlettered Christian and the man who knows more than something of theology. Langland's concern here is to suggest that

> none [are] sonner saved, ne sadder of bileve
> Than plowmen and pastours and povere commune laborers,
> Souteres and shepherdes – swiche lewed juttes. . . .

(B X 456–8)

Guided only by Conscience and Kynde Wit, Piers comes to Truth and serves him *trewely* in a life of *lele* labour. Kynde Wit and Conscience institute the life of labour, and they also guide the individual in his moral life. The claim for Kynde Wit is thus thoroughgoing, and the moral competence of the *kynde* could hardly be greater.[53]

This is the high point of *kynde wit*'s fortunes in the poem, the point at which Langland invests the greatest confidence in the concept. After Ymaginatif's strictures Kynde Wit experiences a recovery and is instrumental in the organisation of the society over which Conscience presides at the end of the poem, but what it can achieve in the company of Conscience (after a dalliance, it appears, with Clergie, Conscience returns to the company of the unlettered and Kynde Wit) is now seen to be severely at risk from the forces of evil, who indeed cause the collapse of Conscience's society. Langland, I think, never completely recovers his earlier extreme optimism regarding what Kynde Wit can accomplish. And at the very end of the poem, Conscience is alone without Kynde Wit, being the only thing able, it seems, to continue the search for Piers, the only human resource which remains effective to the last in the battle against evil,[54] rather as it

---

[53] Coleman (1981), p. 100ff. sees Piers as the natural man able in a strong sense to win salvation partly through his own efforts. Coleman finds a relevant context for *Piers Plowman* in the writings of the Ockhamite *'moderni'* theologians. Some of their positions are open to a charge of Pelagianism (a charge levelled by Thomas Bradwardine in his *De Causa Dei contra Pelagianos*); for instance, it is claimed that God will not deny grace to the man who does what he can to pursue the good *ex puris naturalibus*. Coleman reads Piers' journey to Truth in this light: first Piers follows the Ten Commandments naturally, after which he is rewarded with grace. I doubt, however, that it is necessary to suppose that the following of the commandments occurs without prevenient grace – one can take the grace of which Piers speaks to be *sanctifying* grace, through which one might think it appropriate that Truth's *manoir* should be gained. (It should also be noted that access to the *manoir* is not necessarily going to be granted: 'And *if* Grace graunte thee to go in in this wise' B V 605.) The point I would wish to stress is that Langland thinks that one knows what one has to do through Kynde Wit and Conscience. Kynde Wit's role is to instruct, and knowing what one has to do is not the same as doing it. But it may well be that the theological debate to which Coleman refers the poem is of relevance: as will become apparent, I think Langland may come to suspect that the emphasis he places on *kynde wit* in the early part of the poem smacks of Pelagianism. See further below, p 34.

[54] This is not to say that Conscience is perfect and does not make mistakes – he permits the Friars entry to Unity at the end of the poem. But Conscience by his very nature is always trying to make the right decisions. It should perhaps be acknowledged that we cannot be sure that the ending of B XX represents Langland's 'last analysis'; nevertheless, the treatment of *kynde wit* in C does not suggest that it would have been rehabilitated had Langland revised B XIX and XX. See note 61.

alone will at the last be undestroyed by Kynde (B XX 150–1). In their last analyses of their universes, perhaps, both God and Langland do not have a part for Kynde Wit to play.

Piers, the *kynde wit*ted man, organises a society grounded in labour – as such it is reminiscent of Kynde Wit's society in the Prologue. At the beginning of Passus B VII it appears that this society has been utterly validated by Truth's message and the pardon He offers, which make the pilgrimage that had been proposed (a pilgrimage which had in any case taken on the configurations of the life of honest labour) unnecessary.[55] But, always adept at finding structures proposed as solutions unsatisfactory, Langland (in A and B) has Piers tear the pardon and turn to a life of prayers and penance. The tearing of the pardon is, of course, a notorious crux in the poem, but I think it can safely be said that Piers sees a need for a change of life. The life he has constructed for himself to this point no longer satisfies him. Why he now feels this is a matter to which I shall return, but I should like to suggest at this stage that Kynde Wit, which instructed Piers about the path to Truth and which seems ultimately responsible for the institution of the life of labour over which Piers presides, is deeply implicated in the unsatisfactoriness that Piers perceives in the life he has been leading. It may be because Kynde Wit is implicated in this way that the idea is eventually reappraised in Ymaginatif's discourse.

One of the tasks Ymaginatif sets himself is to correct Will on the question of the use of Clergie, which Will had declared profitless at the end of Passus B X. Ymaginatif's defence of Clergie is conducted very much with an eye to Kynde Wit, and one might wonder why. There is no need to define the limitations of Kynde Wit in order to make clear the importance of Clergie. One senses that so much attention is given to Kynde Wit because claims implicitly made for it need to be refuted. Those claims lie in what Will says about the greater likelihood simple labouring folk have of being saved than do *clerkes*:

> none [are] sonner saved, ne sadder of bileve
> Than plowmen and pastours and povere commune laborers,
> Souteres and shepherdes – swiche lewed juttes
> Percen with a Paternoster the paleys of hevene
> And passen purgatorie penauncelees at hir hennes partyng
> Into the blisse of paradis for hir pure bileve,
> That inparfitly here knewe and ek lyvede.

(B X 456–62)

In the frustration he now feels Will, and perhaps Langland with him, seems to be harking back nostalgically to Piers' society and its ethos, to the life of

---

[55] For a discussion of the development of the second vision of the poem see J. A. Burrow, 'The Action of Langland's Second Vision', *Essays in Criticism*, 15 (1965), 247–68.

honest labour, as an ideal which offers some certain ground.[56] We should, I suspect, recall that Piers' life and society owed everything to the instruction of Kynde Wit, but even if we do not, Will's invocation of the poor unlearned labourer still acts as Kynde Wit's challenge to Clergie, just because a life that rejects Clergie has to run itself with Kynde Wit as its guide (that they are natural alternatives is suggested by Piers' contraposition of them as he announces that he knows Truth).

This recrudescence of the ideal of labour is surely rather problematic for Langland, for Piers, the exemplar of goodness, has changed his life so as to move away from it. Yet here is the old ideal obstinately reasserting itself. That A appears to break down at this point is some indication that Will, overwrought and unreliable as he may be, is not offering a straw man for the easy demolition of his interlocutors. When the B version continues from this point, it perhaps manages to condemn by its fruits the fatalism which Will had professed (B X 369ff.) in response to Clergie's theologising: Will's life is given over to Fortune and loses moral purpose (B XI 3ff.). But this does not impinge upon what Will says about 'plowmen and pastours' at B X 456–62. Indeed, in the Trajan sequence of Passus B XI much is said that only tends to confirm his claims. The commendation of 'leel love and lyvyng in truthe' (161) would fit the old Piers very well, whilst the extolling of patient poverty (230ff.) takes one back to Will's 'povere commune laborers', and the affirmation that *Fides sua* will save the prostitute (216–7) reminds one of Will's claim that the labourers will be saved through 'pure bileve'. And there is also, of course, Trajan's emphatically anti-clerkly stance and status. It begins to look as though Langland's way out of the impasse the labour ideal's return had created was to endorse that ideal, though emphasising at the same time the importance of patience and not insisting on achievement of the good life, perhaps in deference to a sense in Piers that doing well is impossible and to his change of life towards a more spiritual mode.

But what the ideal claims is that Kynde Wit is competent to keep one in touch with God, that there is no need for Clergie. The *Myddelerthe* episode can either be seen as a testing or a failed affirmation of this claim. Will is told 'wit for to take' (B XI 322) through an inspection of the wonders of the world (this I think is the beginning of the Ymaginatif's later conception of *kynde wit* as '*quod vidimus*'), without recourse to *clergie*, in order that he shall love his Creator. But the vision on *Myddelerthe* does not reach its proposed conclusion, for Will comes to question God's purposes as he witnesses the unreasonable behaviour of mankind. This perhaps points to a crucial limitation in *kynde wit* uninformed by *clergie*: it is unable to arrive at

---

[56] It should be said that the presentation of the ideal of honest labour undergoes a change from A to B. In the later version Langland seems to be to some extent under the sway of a new ideal of 'preieres and penaunce', but he is still not laying up his trust in full-blown asceticism, as represented later by Patience. See Godden (1984), pp. 135f.

a full conviction of the love of God, and hence unable to bring a man to love him. This incompetence in relation to the Divine will be exploited by Ymaginatif in his consideration of *kynde wit* in the next Passus.

If we take it that Langland is interested in considering the capacities of *kynde wit* in the context of Will's rejection of Clergie, in setting *kynde wit* deliberately against *clergie*, in fact, this may explain why the term now seems to carry different meanings from those it possessed earlier in the poem. Skeat was able to gloss *kynde wit* 'Common Sense' because it seemed to be something all men possessed; when Piers is depicted as the man of *kynde wit* one doubts any claim is being made about his superior intelligence or wisdom. Rather, he is the ordinary man who uses equipment everyone (or at least all Christians) naturally possess to come to Truth. But when Ymaginatif first uses the term, he seems to mean by it high intelligence or wisdom. Ymaginatif cites Aristotle, Hippocrates and Virgil along with Alexander and tells us that

> Catel and kynde wit was combraunce to hem alle. (B XII 45)

'Felice' and 'Rosamounde' are then cited as examples of those undone by their own beauty. In this context *kynde wit* is plainly not something possessed by everyone. Ymaginatif goes on to draw his conclusions:

> So catel and kynde wit acombreth ful manye;
> Wo is hym that hem weldeth but he hem wel despende:
> *Scient[es] et non facient[es] variis flagellis vapulab[un]t.*
> Sapience, seith the Bok, swelleth a mannes soule:
> *Sapiencia inflat &c.*
> And richesse right so, but if the roote be trewe. (B XII 55–8)

It seems to me that the ground for this change has been prepared in Will's *Myddelerthe* vision, where he acquired much knowledge of the natural world, much *kynde wit*, we might say,[57] over and above what all men know. Indeed, though, I think, the reconsideration of *kynde wit* is called forth by the re-entry into the poem of simple ignorant labour as an ideal, an ideal associated in the person of Piers with *kynde wit*,[58] the redefinition of the concept makes it possible for *kynde wit* to stand in contrast to the *lewednesse* of simple ignorant labour at B XII 156–9.

> I took ful good hede
> How thow contrariedest clergie with crabbede wordes,
> How that lewed men lightloker than lettrede were saved,
> Than clerkes or kynde witted men, of Cristene peple.

[57] I suspect that *kynde wit* throughout this section of the B text is a body of knowledge. But Langland may suppose the faculty *kynde wit* '(high) natural intelligence' to be intimately involved in acquiring natural wisdom, so it would still be possible to understand, say, the *kynde wit* Virgil and his fellows have as a faculty.

[58] The *kynde witted* Piers is, I think, *lewed* in the way the workers Will invokes at the end of B X are. We learn that his being 'lettred' (B VII 132) is a result not of the study of books, but of moral living (B VII 133–4). Piers' wisdom is one available to the illiterate peasant.

But this is not the only change undergone by the concept of *kynde wit* as a result of the focusing on the contrast between it and *clergie*. I have argued that *kynde wit* in the first part of the poem is not to be thought of as unillumined by divine revelation, but here it is noticeable that its representatives are pagan (though it may be that Solomon, who is mentioned just before Aristotle, Hippocrates and Virgil, also represents *kynde wit* – see B XII 40–4). When Langland goes on to counterpose *clergie* as well as *kynde wit* against grace, it seems that he is thinking of *kynde wit* as something available to all men including pagans through an inspection of the world, but of *clergie* as knowing more than *quod vidimus*, 'what we have seen'. *Quod scimus* 'what we know', are the truths of revelation, truths not to be gathered from any amount of consideration of the natural world:[59]

> Clergie and kynde wit cometh of sighte and techyng,
> As the Book bereth witnesse to burnes that can rede:
> *Quod scimus loquimur, quod vidimus testamur.*
> Of *quod scimus* cometh clergie, a konnynge of hevene,
> And of *quod vidimus* cometh kynde wit, of sighte of diverse peple.
> Ac grace is a gifte of God, and of greet love spryngeth;
> Knew nevere clerk how it cometh forth, ne kynde wit the weyes:
> *Nescit aliquis unde venit aut quo vadit &c.*
>
> (B XII 64–9a)

The *quod scimus* / *quod vidimus* distinction is drawn from St John's Gospel, chapter 3, verse 11. This, with verse 12, runs as follows:

> Amen, amen, dico tibi, quia quod scimus loquimur, et quod vidimus testamur, et testimonium nostrum non accipitis.
> Si terrena dixi vobis, et non creditis: quomodo, si dixero vobis coelestia, creditis?

Apparently Langland took the seeing / knowing opposition as parallel to that between *terrena* and *coelestia*. *Clergie* is in some sense 'of hevene' and *kynde wit* of the earth. This does not encourage one to suppose that *kynde wit* of itself offers access to Truth.[60]

[59] However, John Lawlor, *Piers Plowman: An Essay in Criticism* (London, 1962), p. 116, finds that 'the ground of "Clergy" and "Kind Wit" is natural knowledge and natural observation, *quod scimus* and *quod vidimus*'.

[60] The C text differs considerably from B at this point:

> Ac clergie cometh bote of syhte and kynde wit of sterres,
> As to be bore or bygete in such a constillacioun,
> That with wexeth therof and oþer wordes bothe.
> *Vultus huius seculi sunt subiecti vultibus celestibus.*
> So grace is a gifte of god and kynde wit a chaunce
> And clergie a connynge of kynde wittes techyng.
>
> (C XIV 30–4)

In C Langland appears to suppose that both *quod scimus* and *quod vidimus* are *terrena* as opposed to *coelestia*. He still thinks of *clergie* as a *connynge* (*quod scimus*), but it no longer has the high status accorded to it in B on the strength of its association with *coelestia*. It is now thought to derive from *kynde wit* and is, in the last analysis, a matter of astrological *chaunce*. In

The passage affirms the superiority of grace to both *clergie* and *kynde wit*. But even the lowest of the three, *kynde wit*, is, like *clergie*, not without merit:

> Ac yet is clergie to comende, and kynde wit bothe,
> And namely clergie for Cristes love, that of clergie is roote.[61]

> (B XII 70–1)

Christ, Ymaginatif continues, saved the woman taken in adultery through *clergie*, which shows that *clergie* comforts the penitent, as it does in the Eucharist where *clergie* is necessary to turn the bread into Christ's body:

> Forthi I counseille thee for Cristes sake, clergie that thow lovye,
> For kynde wit is of his kyn and neighe cosynes bothe
> To Oure Lord, leve me – forthi love hem, I rede.
> For bothe ben as mirours to amenden oure defautes,
> And lederes for lewed men and for lettred bothe.

> (B XII 92–6)

The connective *For* in the second line seems a little strange, since Ymaginatif has just stated that *clergie* is superior to *kynde wit*. How, then, can *kynde wit* lend *clergie* credibility? I think Ymaginatif is making an *ad hominem* appeal to Will: Will has cause to love *clergie* because *clergie* is by no means inimical to *kynde wit*, which Will already approves. If this explanation is correct,

---

B *kynde wit*'s coming 'of sighte' involved inspection of the world and was differentiated from the *quod scimus* of revelation. In C *clergie*'s coming 'of syhte' seems to involve reading books containing the divine revelation:

> For as a man may nat se þat misseth his yes
> No more can no clerk but if hit come of bokes.
> Al-þeiȝ men made bokis god was here mayster
> And þe seynt spirit þe saumplare and said what men sholde wryte.

> (C XIV 44–7)

There remains a differentiation between *kynde wit* and *clergie*, for all that they may be considered *terrena* in opposition to grace. Thus it can be said:

> And ȝut is clergie to comende for Cristes loue more
> Then eny connyng of kynde wit but clergi hit reule.

> (C XIV 35–6)

When Pearsall (1978) on C XIV 30, p. 236, refers to *clergie* as learning and explains, 'Learning comes only from what we have seen or learnt empirically', I am not sure that he recognises the distinction between the 'connynge of kynde wittes techyng' that is *clergie* and other kinds of 'connyng of kynde wit'.

[61] The C version (C XIV 35–6, quoted in the previous note) is much less positive about *kynde wit*. One can detect a diminution in the status of *kynde wit* in this portion of the C text. In addition to the change just noted, whilst in B Ymaginatif's summary of what Will said about the chances of salvation of the *lewed* being better than those of the *lettrede* (B XII 156–9) includes *kynde wit* as well as *clergie*, C speaks of 'connynge clerkes of kynde vnderstondynge' (XIV 102), thus removing *kynde wit* as a separate category. Again, whereas B XII 126ff. contrasts *clergie* and *kynde wit*, the equivalent C passage, XIV 70ff., speaks of how 'Kynde-wittede men han a clergie by hemslue', which means that the focus is on two kinds of *clergie*. C also alters B so as to ascribe the possession of *kynde wit* to animals; it is something they have in common with men (see C XIV 157, 162f.). This perhaps detracts from the dignity of *kynde wit*.

further support is provided for the suggestion that Will's elevation of simple labourers above *clerkes* is an elevation of *kynde wit*.[62]

However this may be, in the last quoted passage *kynde wit* is vindicated as a moral educator. One wonders whether the last line here suggests that *kynde wit* leads the unlettered and *clergie* the learned, or whether both classes of people are offered guidance by each of the forces, but in any case a pleasing accommodation of both the opposed kinds of knowledge has apparently been made. It comes as something of a surprise, then, when Ymaginatif turns back to an attack on the value of *kynde wit*:

> Forthi lakke thow nevere logik, lawe ne hise custumes,
> Ne countreplede clerkes – I counseille thee for evere!
> For as a man may noght see that mysseth hise eighen,
> Na moore kan no clerk but if he caughte it first thorugh bokes..
> Although men made bokes, God was the maister,
> And Seint Spirit the samplarie, and seide what men sholde write.
> And right as sight serveth a man to se the heighe strete,
> Right so lereth lettrure lewed men to reson.
> And as a blynd man in bataille bereth wepne to fighte,
> And hath noon hap with his ax his enemy to hitte,
> Na moore kan a kynde witted man, but clerkes hym teche,
> Come, for al his kynde wit, to Cristendom and be saved –
> Which is the cofre of Cristes tresor, and clerkes kepe the keyes,
> To unloken it at hir likyng, and to the lewed peple
> Yyve mercy for hire mysdedes, if men it wole aske
> Buxomliche and benigneliche, and bidden it of grace.      (B XII 97–112)

Langland's simile of the blind warrior perhaps suggests that *kynde wit* does have some desire to join the fight against evil, but that its efforts are directionless, lacking the orientation a knowledge of the Christian revelation would give it. Christians can deal effective blows against evil through penance, for the efficacy of which (an efficacy affirmed in the Christian revelation) a clergy capable of mediating sacramental grace is required. The last part of the passage describes the role of the clergy once Christendom has been reached, but earlier we see how the *kynde wit*ted man has to be informed of the Christian revelation. Though 'lewed men' may represent a third category additional to the *kynde wit*ted man and *clerkes*, it is still accurate to see the *kynde wit*ted man as *lewed* of *reson*, in the sense of not knowing the truth, and as such unable to be saved. Here Langland's analysis of the capacities of *kynde wit* leads him to see it as natural wisdom (or natural reason) unillumined by divine revelation. Earlier in the poem *kynde wit* had functioned in a Christian society and seemed to have some knowledge of the Christian revelation. Will's assault on *clergie* and implicit support for *kynde wit* following what seems to be the discovery of the unsatisfactoriness of a way of life in which the guidance of *kynde wit* was

---

[62] Even though, as we have seen, *kynde wit* is transformed into something that distances it from the ideal of the simple labourer.

central have, I think, led to a focus on what *kynde wit* can do on its own, and this has in turn produced a rather different understanding of *kynde wit*, in which its knowledge of revelation, which, in fact, it always owed, in a sense, to *clergie*, has been taken from it.

Shortly after this passage, Ymaginatif links its incapacity to lead to salvation to the earthboundness of *kynde wit*, which comes 'of sighte' and is limited to what is *huius mundi*, knowing nothing of Christ:

> Forthi I conseille alle creatures no clergie to dispise, . . . .
> For clergie is kepere under Crist of hevene;
> [Com] ther nevere no knyght but clergie hym made.
> Ac kynde wit cometh of alle kynnes sightes –
> Of briddes and of beestes, [of blisse and of sorwe],
> Of tastes of truthe and [oft] of deceites.[63]
> [Olde] lyveris toforn us useden to marke[64]
> The selkouthes that thei seighen, hir sones for to teche,
> And helden it an heigh science hir wittes to knowe.
> Ac thorugh hir science soothly was nevere no soule ysaved,
> Ne broght by hir bokes to blisse ne to joye;
> For alle hir kynde knowyng com but of diverse sightes.[65]
> Patriarkes and prophetes repreveden hir science,
> And seiden hir wordes ne hir wisdomes was but a folye;
> As to the clergie of Crist, counted it but a trufle:
> *Sapiencia huius mundi stultitia est apud Deum.*
>
> (B XII 121, 126–39a)

This is not to say that *kynde wit* of the sort produced by pagan sages is completely worthless. Contemplation of the birds and the beasts can yield useful material in the moral realm:

> Ac of briddes and of beestes men by olde tyme
> Ensamples token and termes, as telleth thise poetes,
> And that the faireste fowel foulest engendreth,
> And feblest fowel of flight is that fleeth or swymmeth.
> And that is the pecock and the pehen – proude riche men thei bitokneth.
>
> (B XII 236–40)

[63] It should be recalled that in his vision on *Myddelerthe* Will's attention was very much on 'briddes and beestes', which encourages one to suppose that the knowledge he gains there is indeed a *kynde wit*.

[64] For this line C substitutes

> Kynde-wittede men han a clergie by hemsulue;
> Of cloudes and of costumes they contreuede mony thynges
> And markede hit in here manere and mused þeron to knowe.
>
> (C XIV 72–4)

Pearsall comments (p. 237), '*cloudes* and *costomes* ('customs') could refer to the two domains of natural science and moral philosophy'.

[65] This is one point at which *kynde wit* and *kynde knowynge* may be identified (it seems to be on the strength of this passage that Quirk (1953), p. 184, finds the concepts identical in *Piers Plowman*), though I think that the ideas are normally distinct (see Chapter 2). In fact, even in this passage *kynde knowyng* may mean 'proper knowledge'; the thought would then be that the best pagan philosophers could do by way of knowledge was only derived from 'diverse sightes' and as such inefficacious for salvation.

The trouble is that this kind of moral teaching,[66] laudable though it may be, does not suffice to bring men to salvation. As we shall see in considering Will's experience on *Myddelerthe*, there are difficulties even for the Christian in using the sight of creation productively towards salvation.

We might then have an analysis of *kynde wit* in its new guise according to Augustinian ideas: the moral enterprise of those living without the Christian revelation is worthless for salvation.[67] But Ymaginatif's oscillations of attitude towards *kynde wit* are not finished. Despite his earlier remarks, towards the end of the Passus he expresses uncertainty over the question of the salvation of Aristotle, hoping, nevertheless, that God will save him and others because they have given mankind such effective moral teaching. This is not quite to say that these figures will be saved through *kynde wit*, but when Ymaginatif goes on to counter Will's contention (B XII 275–7) – and Will, ironically enough, now rests his view on the authority of Christian *clerkes* – that 'neither Sarsens ne Jewes' will be saved with the example of Trajan, he does seem to be suggesting that the good life lived without the benefit of revelation may win salvation:

> Ac truthe that trespased nevere ne traversed ayeins his lawe,
> But lyveth as his lawe techeth and leveth ther be no bettre,
> (And if ther were, he wolde amende) and in swich wille deieth –
> Ne wolde nevere trewe God but trewe truthe were allowed.     (B XII 285–8)

What follows may suggest that Ymaginatif is not sure of what he has just said, and indeed the fluctuations of his attitude indicate that Langland himself is uncertain on the question of the righteous heathen.[68] At the bottom of

---

[66] Later in the Passus (B XII 262–7) Aristotle (replaced by Porphyry and Plato at C XIV 189) is credited with having made a moral *ensample* of the lark.

[67] The *locus classicus* is *De Civitate Dei* V. On Augustine's views see, e.g., P. Delhaye, *Permanence du Droit Naturel* Analecta Mediaevalia Namurcensia 10 (Louvain/Lille/Montreal, 1960), pp. 54–5.

[68] The text at the end of Ymaginatif's discourse is uncertain. At B XII 289 Schmidt (1987) reads

> And wheither it worth or noght worth, the bileve is gret of truthe, . . . .

whilst Kane and Donaldson reconstruct their B XII 291 as follows:

> And wheiþer it worþ [of truþe] or noȝt, [þe] worþ [of] bileue is gret, . . . .

Schmidt, p. 286, disputes the reconstruction on theological grounds, arguing that the sense of the line cannot be, as Kane and Donaldson (p. 209) suggest, 'And the intrinsic value of faith is great, whether it actually comes to be faith in the true religion . . . or not', since 'faith was seen as a divine gift and so must be, if only implicitly, faith in the true religion.' G. Whatley, '*Piers Plowman* B 12. 277–94: Notes on Language, Text, and Theology', *MP*, (1984), 1–12 has argued for the Kane and Donaldson text against Schmidt. Whatever the case, the point remains that Langland himself is uncertain on the status of the righteous heathen. On this topic see, e.g., T. P. Dunning, 'Langland and the Salvation of the Heathen', *MAE*, 12 (1943), 45–54.; G. H. Russell, 'The Salvation of the Heathen: The Exploration of a Theme in *Piers Plowman*', *Journal of the Warburg and Courtauld Institutes*, 29 (1966) 101–16; Coleman (1981),; Pamela Gradon, '*Trajanus Redivivus*: Another look at Trajan in *Piers Plowman*', in *Middle English Studies presented to Norman Davis*, ed. Douglas Gray and E. G. Stanley (Oxford, 1983), pp. 93–114; G. Whatley, 'The Uses of Hagiography: The Legend of Pope Gregory and the Emperor Trajan in the Middle Ages', *Viator*, 15 (1984), 25–63.

this issue for Langland may lie his inability to surrender the status he initially accorded *kynde wit*. Trajan after all tells us

> al the clergie under Crist ne myghte me cracche fro helle
> But oonliche love and leautee and my laweful domes.
>
> (B XI 144–5)

We should here remember Kynde Wit's insistence on law and *leaute* and how in A he was a leader in the society of love envisaged by Conscience. Ymaginatif's final remarks have the effect of returning the debate between *clergie* and *kynde wit* to the melting-pot. It is to be noted too that in the next Passus Conscience leaves Clergie behind and goes on pilgrimage with the unlearned Patience.

Langland reverts to the problem of the salvation of the heathen later in the poem, and the following passage from the discourse of Liberum Arbitrium in C seems to run counter to Ymaginatif's views at the end of Passus B XII:

> Hit may be so þat Sarresynes haen such a manere charite,
> Louen as by lawe of kynde oure lord god almyhty.
> Hit is kyndly thyng creature his creatour to honoure,
> For þer is no man þat mynde hath þat ne meketh him and bysecheth
> To þat lord þat hym lyf lente, lyflode hym sende.
> Ac many manere men þer ben, as Sarresynes and Iewes,
> Louyeth nat þat lord aryht as by þe Legende *Sanctorum*
> And lyuen oute of lele byleue for they leue on a mene.
> A man þat hihte Makameth for Messie they hym holdeth
> And aftur his leryng they lyue and by lawe of kynde,
> And when kynde hath his cours and no contrarie fyndeth
> Thenne is lawe ylefte and leute vnknowe.
> *Beaute sanz bounte* blessed was hit neuere
> Ne kynde *sanz cortesie* in no contreye is preysed.
>
> (C XVII 151–64)

The *mynde* in line 154 seems to allow one to understand the love of the creator as something that comes about through *kynde wit*; certainly the natural law, which can be perceived through natural reason, is orthodoxly understood to require love of God. But the *kynde* is not enough; it needs to be cultivated so that correct belief in Christ can be reached, and it is not sufficient of itself to produce *lawe* and *leute*.

In this passage Langland does not want to make much of the claims of anything *kynde* in the sphere of morality, and it seems that whatever the *Sarresynes* know naturally does not have sufficient power to hold them back from the evil to which their *kynde* conduces. (One might contrast the confident claims made for *kynde wit* in relation to *lawe* and *leaute* in the

Prologue.[69]) The loss of confidence in *kynde wit* seems to have gone a stage further than in Ymaginatif's discourse in B (in C it is noticeable that Ymaginatif is less well disposed towards *kynde wit* than he is in B[70]). But this passage, though additionally casting aspersions on *kynde wit*'s moral capacity, resembles earlier passages in its insistence that *kynde wit* fails to lead to Christ. In the earlier passages its incapacity to lead to salvation was the result of an attachment to this world and a detachment from Christ. I have suggested that the examination of *kynde wit* Ymaginatif conducts is connected with the discovery that what one might call the *kynde wit* ethos of the society of the half-acre is unsatisfactory. This produces a re-assessment of *kynde wit* which shifts the sense in which the term is taken. But it is, I think, possible to see problems with the *kynde wit* of the earlier part of the poem which can be stated in terms of attachment to the world and detachment from Christ.

Having torn the pardon Piers says that he is not going to be so concerned about his 'bely joye', and that he will make his plough one of prayers and penance (B VII 118–20). He seems to think his efforts have been too much focused on the material. We have seen that *kynde wit* is much concerned with the production of food and related matters: on its first entry into the poem it is associated with *husbondrie* and preaches moderate consumption (as he tears the pardon Piers would, one suspects, have nothing but scorn for *husbondrie*). The institution of society in which Kynde Wit plays such an important role has at its root the production of food. Again, as I have mentioned, a C text passage sees God's provision of *kynde wit* as the provision of a means of physical survival (either for the individual or the species):

> He [Kynde] tauhte þe tortle to trede, the pocok to cauke,
> And Adam and Eue and alle othere bestes
> A cantel of kynde wyt here kynde to saue.　　(C XIV 161–3)

It is not that Kynde Wit is exclusively concerned with ensuring physical survival: he preaches the contemplative as well as the active life, and the life of labour in any case clearly has a moral value. But Langland comes, for a time, at least, to see the good life as laid up in prayers and penance rather than in the life of labour.[71] Patience is the figure who enshrines most clearly

---

[69] Kynde Wit's shaping *lawe* and *leaute* does not, of course, make it inevitable that these will be followed in practice, so there is no actual contradiction between what is said in the Prologue and in this later C passage. But the enthusiastic attitude to what is available by *kynde* has been very much modified.

[70] See note 61.

[71] See Godden (1984). Godden argues that the phrase 'preieres and penaunce' denotes a way of life, a life of eremitical asceticism (pp. 132–3), and that this life exercises a pull as an ideal on Langland which is in tension with the attraction of the life of labour to him. It should be said that the ideal of labour appears to be revalidated towards the end of the B text, though not to the exclusion of the ascetic life (see B XIX 230ff., especially 237–8 and 249–50) and perhaps not finally and unassailably (see B XX 207–11).

this new vision, and he is prepared to recommend absolute abandonment of concern for the provision of bodily necessities:

Darstow nevere care for corn ne lynnen cloth ne wollen,
Ne for drynke, ne deeth drede, but deye as God liketh,
Or thorugh hunger or thorugh hete – at his wille be it.
For if thow lyvest after his loore, the shorter lif the bettre:
*Si quis amat Christum mundum non diligit istum.*

(B XIV 56–9a)

In such a perspective it may well be that Kynde Wit's concern with the material realm could be construed as over-involvement in this world at the expense of a commitment to God. One might go on to suggest that the reason why Kynde Wit's attention is insufficiently focused on God is because he lacks the trust in Him Patience advocates: deliberate pursuit of the means of survival, besides removing attention from God, might indicate a failure of trust in Him. To erect and inhabit the protective structures of the state might be thought to do likewise – as he abandons (as I take it) his societal role,[72] Piers affirms his trust in God through his first psalm text:

*Si ambulavero in medio umbre mortis*
*Non timebo mala, quoniam tu mecum es.*

(B VII 116–7)

To attempt to live the good life through the structures *kynde wit* provides might also be argued to be heretical, allowing too much significance to what man of himself can do. *Kynde wit* is not a gift of God in the same way that grace is, and to invest as much trust in it as Langland does in the earlier part of the poem is arguably Pelagian. Piers' pardon requires man to do well. What receiving it does to Piers, the hero of the ethos of *kynde wit*, may constitute Langland's repudiation of his implicit claim that the capacity to live the good life is essentially laid up in what is readily available to man in virtue of his *kynde*. Hence the turn to the life of prayers and penance which acknowledges man's complete helplessness, his absolute need for God, and makes no claims for man's capacities in the pursuit of Truth. It is, as we have seen, penance and grace which are beyond *kynde wit*'s reach in Passus B XII.[73]

---

[72] The terms in which Piers describes his new life are somewhat equivocal. But it seems to me that there is a real movement away from the life of labour, not just a re-definition of it, as Robert Adams, 'Piers' Pardon and Langland's Semi-Pelagianism', *Traditio*, 39 (1983), 367–418, argues (p. 405f.).

[73] For a view in some respects similar to my own see Denise Baker, 'The Pardons of *Piers Plowman*', *Neuphilologische Mitteilungen*, 85 (1984), 462–72; also her earlier 'From Plowing to Penitence: *Piers Plowman* and 14th century Theology', *Speculum*, 55 (1980), 715–25. Unlike Baker, I would be inclined to see such problems in *Piers Plowman* as the tearing of the pardon as evidence of difficulties and uncertainties felt by Langland himself rather than as controlled and sophisticated authorial strategies. Adams (1983) seeks to counter Baker and others who take what he calls a 'revisionist' position over the pardon.

In various ways, then, the *kynde wit* of the earlier part of the poem may be seen to be insufficiently centred on God, and a feeling that this is so may lie behind Langland's later exposure of *kynde wit*'s deficiencies. That exposure makes explicit what was implicit in Piers' change of life, *kynde wit*'s incapacity to bring man to salvation, and it offers reasons for that incapacity which may be tentatively aligned with difficulties that can be sensed about *kynde wit* in the first part of the poem. I want now to consider some rather more specific limitations from which *kynde wit* suffers, before examining its restoration to a degree of favour later in the poem.

Though *kynde wit* can derive important wisdom from observation of the natural world, it cannot fathom the reasons behind God's disposition of it:

> And so I seye by thee, that sekest after the whyes,
> And aresonedest Reson, a rebukynge as it were,
> And willest of briddes and of beestes and of hir bredyng knowe,
> Why some be alough and some aloft, thi likyng it were;
> And of the floures in the fryth and of hire faire hewes –
> Wherof thei cacche hir colours so clere and so brighte,
> And of the stones and of the sterres – thow studiest, as I leve,
> How evere beest outher brid hath so breme wittes. . . .
>     Clergie ne Kynde Wit ne knew nevere the cause,
> Ac Kynde knoweth the cause hymself and no creature ellis.
>
>                           (B XII 217–26)

In the following passage *kynde wit* is again puzzled over God's activity:

> Ac God is of a wonder wille, by that kynde wit sheweth,
> To yyve many men his mercymonye er he it have deserved.
> Right so fareth God by some riche:
>
>                           (B XIV 125–7)

Patience goes on to acknowledge (B XIV 144ff.) that God will even give the right-living rich man double reward, an arrangement presumably equally upsetting to *kynde wit*'s preconceptions of how things should be done. But God's dealings with man are not bound by the prescriptions of *kynde wit*, however binding on men these may be.[74] *Kynde wit*'s bafflement reveals how its perceptions need the support of the revelation entrusted to Clergie (though, as we have just seen, Clergie itself does not have all the answers). Kynde Wit's incapacity to grasp unaided the divine reality is revealed again over the Trinity. The Samaritan requires Will to accept the doctrine of the Trinity announced by Abraham:

> And if conscience carpe therayein, or kynde wit eyther,
> Or eretikes with arguments – thyn hond thow hem shewe:
> For God is after an hand – yheer now and knowe it.
>
>                           (B XVII 137–9)

---

[74] This passage seems to me to show that God is not, in Langland's conception, constrained by considerations of justice even when being merciful, though Stokes (1984) claims otherwise (see, e.g., p. 94).

The long unfolding of the doctrine of the Trinity in terms of the parts of the hand follows (it is an exposition accommodated to a reliance on *quod vidimus*). The doctrine of the Trinity may well not appear to make sense, and it is therefore likely that the natural understanding will reject it, whether natural understanding be opposed to Christian revelation or to specialised theological knowledge. And Conscience might not unreasonably decide not to believe something that Kynde Wit says cannot be the case: we have seen how Conscience takes Kynde Wit as its teacher on other occasions. But the lack of understanding testifies to a limitation, and the failure here envisaged for the partnership of Kynde Wit and Conscience, the first time this combination is found wanting, points forward to the end of the poem where Conscience and Kynde Wit fail to prevent the overthrow of Unity.[75] There, as here, a need for the guidance of Clergie makes itself felt – Passus B XII has left its legacy. Kynde Wit can still be supposed capable of sound moral judgement in the sphere of society:

> If knyghthod and kynde wit, and the commune and conscience
> Togideres love leelly, leveth it wel, ye bisshopes –
> The lordshipe of londes [lese ye shul for evere],
> And lyven as *Levitici*, as Oure Lord yow techeth:
> *Per primicias et decimas &c.*

(B XV 551–4a)

and indeed Langland seems to return to a sense that the good life can be pursued within society when he makes the various crafts gifts of the Holy Ghost in Passus B XIX,[76] (this revaluation of society may have to do with Kynde Wit's resumption of important functions in the attempt to live the good life), but *kynde wit* now lies under the shadow of its inferiority to *clergie*, as its treatment in the final phase of the poem clearly testifies.

The control of *kynde wit* by *clergie* is something that Piers himself recommends when he lays down the procedures for living the good life in the community which Grace institutes in Passus B XIX. Grace has given Piers four *stottes*, the four great Doctors of the Church, to support the ploughing of the Evangelists. In the land thus prepared the Cardinal Virtues are sown:

> Thise foure sedes Piers sew, and siththe he dide hem harewe
> With Olde Lawe and Newe Lawe, that love myghte wexe
> Among thise foure vertues, and vices destruye.
> 'For comunliche in contrees cammokes and wedes
> Foulen the fruyt in the feld ther thei growen togideres;
> And so doon vices vertues – [f]orthi,' quod Piers,
> 'Hareweth alle that konneth kynde wit by conseil of thise doctours,
> And tilieth after hir techynge the cardynale vertues.'

(B XIX 311–8)

---

[75] The C text here does not mention Conscience, so that all the implicit blame falls upon Kynde Wit. This is perhaps in line with the devaluation of Kynde Wit in the C text which I mentioned above. See note 61.

[76] On this see Godden (1984), pp. 150–2.

Langland may be suggesting that men have a natural understanding of how to be virtuous and a natural capacity to produce at least the beginnings of virtue – the Cardinal Virtues can, after all, orthodoxly be understood to be natural – but if this is the case, the harvest of virtue, it seems, can only be secured with the help of the learning of the Church.[77] Having on his first appearance made the highest claims for Kynde Wit and Conscience Piers seems now, at the end of the poem, to acknowledge that the maintenance of virtue requires more than these two on their own can produce. Langland's initial enthusiasm for *kynde wit* has been somewhat dampened in the course of the poem.

Yet for all that, Kynde Wit at the end of the poem is still a force to be reckoned with on the side of virtue. The search for the good life within society has been revalidated, the sponsorship of society and its various crafts by Grace forestalling, perhaps, the charge of Pelagianism, and indicating that society can be God-centred. Kynde Wit is found, as earlier in the poem, instructing on how the community should proceed for its own welfare. *Kynde wit* seems to have resumed its earlier identity, in fact, in large measure, shaking off the redefinition imposed upon it in Passus B XII. Kynde Wit is now once more functioning within a Christian society and, as on his earlier appearances in the poem, it seems that what he does has a specifically Christian quality. Once more too he is presented as Conscience's teacher. But this time the direction of his instruction is explicitly religious: the labour he demands is directed to exclusively spiritual ends. We might even say that we have a version of the contemplative life that Kynde Wit was earlier said to encourage, but which rather took second place to the life of honest labour and its commitment to the business of staying alive. Here no one could suggest that Kynde Wit produced a society which was not concentrated on God:

> And thanne kam Kynde Wit Conscience to teche,
> And cryde, and comaundede alle Cristene peple
> For to delven and dyche depe aboute Unitee
> That Holy Chirche stode in [holynesse], as it a pyl weere.
>     Conscience comaundede tho alle Cristene to delve,
> And make a muche moot that myghte ben a strengthe
> To helpe Holy Chirche and hem that it kepeth. . . .
>     Ther nas no Cristene creature that kynde wit hadde –
> Save sherewes one swich as I spak of –
> That he ne halp a quantite holynesse to wexe:
> Some by bedes biddynge and some by pilgrymage
> And other pryve penaunce, and somme thorugh penyes delynge.
>                                   (B XIX 363–9, 375–9)

[77] On the Cardinal Virtues see Schmidt (1987) on B XIX 276, pp. 354–5. These virtues are not innate, but are acquirable without the help of grace, though they may also be infused (see M. W. Bloomfield, *Piers Plowman as a Fourteenth Century Apocalypse* (New Brunswick, 1961) p. 134).

This is to suggest that there is a basic understanding in a Christian society – at least when it feels the pressure of evil acutely – that holiness should be cultivated through the performance of certain actions. The actions Kynde Wit advises are no longer to do with secular law and justice, or with work in the fields: we seem rather to have a withdrawal from worldly business to concentrate on matters spiritual. Perhaps one should not say withdrawal, since the life of worldly affairs does appear to have been justified in the gifts of the Holy Ghost, but at least the focus of life is now explicitly spiritual – *ne solliciti sitis* in practice, perhaps, albeit in less radical a form than Patience had advised.[78]

Even though worries over *kynde wit* have developed in the course of the poem, that the Holy Ghost should give the natural Cardinal Virtues[79] and also be responsible for the ordinary mundane skills of the various crafts and professions, skills which were in the Prologue in the province of Kynde Wit, indicates that Langland still takes a highly favourable view of the natural endowment and abilities of mankind. The natural is brought into very close association with the divine, and this is a pattern evident in Langland's identification of God as Kynde and his treatment of *kynde*ness, which I examine in later chapters.

It is the Friars who eventually bring about the downfall of Unity. Conscience attempts to resist them with a consideration advanced by Kynde Wit (again Kynde Wit is Conscience's teacher):

> 'Monkes and moniales and alle men of religion –
> Hir ordre and hir reule wole to han a certein noumbre;
> Of lewed and of lered the lawe wole and asketh
> A certein for a certein – save oonliche of freres!
> Forthi,' quod Conscience, 'by Crist! kynde wit me telleth
> It is wikked to wage yow – ye wexen out of noumbre!
> Forthi I wolde witterly that ye were in the registre
> And youre noumbre under notarie sygne, and neither mo ne lasse!'
>
> (B XX 264–72)

Lines occurring just before this passage perhaps indicate what Langland has in mind when he speaks of Kynde Wit here:

> And if ye coveite cure, Kynde wol yow telle
> That in mesure God made alle manere thynges,
> And sette it at a certein and at a siker noumbre,

---

[78] Patience appears to counsel absolute abandonment of any concern for bodily welfare (B XIV 50ff.), though Martin (1979), pp. 135–7, 140, suggests that this idealising absolutist stance cannot be sustained for very long in the face of Langland's suspicion of such stances. Frank (1957), pp. 31–3, has shown that *ne solliciti sitis* was frequently understood not as a call to renunciation of all material concerns, but as a warning against excessive attachment to the material realm.

[79] Bloomfield (1961), p. 134, wonders why the Holy Ghost should be distributing *natural* Cardinal Virtues, and suggests that we should understand the Cardinal Virtues here to be infused through grace.

And nempnede hem names newe, and noumbrede the sterres:
*Qui numerat multitudinem stellarum et omnibus eis &c.*

(B XX 253–6a)

The suggestion appears to be that observation of God's work in creation shows that God abides by the principle of measure, and the presence of this principle in the natural realm indicates that respect for that principle is incumbent on man as part of the natural law.[80] It seems likely that the Kynde Wit Conscience goes on to invoke has come by its knowledge of the principle of measure through a *sighte*, *quod vidimus*, in accordance with what we learn of it in Passus B XII. This is all very well, but perhaps we should suspect that Kynde Wit's instruction, drawn from what it observes, will not have sufficient power to hold back evil: we learnt of the poverty in respect of salvation of *quod vidimus* in Passus B XII, and what the Christian Will sees on *Myddelerthe* does not bring him to love of God.

Kynde Wit and Conscience are left to defend Unity without Grace and Piers who have departed on their mission of spiritual ploughing. Langland seems to be offering a picture of what man can do towards his salvation without these special presences. There is a further absentee, Clergie. Earlier (B XIII 179ff.), Conscience decided to abandon Clergie and follow Patience, the exemplar of the life of prayers and penance: commitment to this life seems to require the abandonment of Clergie.[81] The setting of Unity in Holiness which is constructed in large measure out of prayers and penance perhaps similarly requires the absence of Clergie. At any rate Clergie is not present. But when Conscience made his decision to follow Patience Clergie warned him (and Conscience accepted the warning) that he would find that he needed Clergie at some stage in the future. So it proves – Conscience calls out for Clergie in the siege of Unity:

Help, Clergie, or ellis I falle
Thorugh inparfite preestes and prelates of Holy Chirche!

(B XX 228–9)

but Clergie does not come, even when Conscience repeats his cry (B XX 376), and Unity, presumably, falls. The corrupt learning of the Friars is an important factor in the fall:

Envye herfore hatede Conscience,
And freres to philosophie he fond hem to scole,
The while Coveitise and Unkyndenesse Conscience assaillede.

(B XX 295–7)

---

[80] This kind of deduction of moral principle from observation of the natural scene is common in contemporary homiletic writing.

[81] On this parting see Martin (1979), pp. 120–2. Conscience projects an ideal vision of a world-transforming coalition made up of himself, Clergie and Patience (B XIII 205ff.). In the imperfect actuality in which the action of the poem is set, however, Patience and Clergie are perhaps incompatible pursuits.

No doubt Langland supposes it is used to justify the dealing out of the cheap grace that drugs the inhabitants of Unity.[82] It is clear that the life of the Church in the world is not secure from the contagion of evil without the learning Clergie possesses. No doubt an absolute security would require also Grace and Piers. But Kynde Wit can provide none of these.

Where Kynde Wit fails at the end of the poem is in the realm of the societal; what falls apart is a community of men trying to hold themselves together in virtue. This is very appropriate to Kynde Wit's abiding concern in the poem with the ordering of societies. This last community is certainly a God-centred one, but it is also a human one and as such unreliable. At the end we are left with Conscience unsupported by any human society going in search of Piers and calling on Kynde and Grace. Human societies, even spiritually orientated ones, are always vulnerable to the assaults of evil. The only human thing in which trust can be laid up is the individual conscience in pursuit of the good life and reliant on God's grace, and even the conscience will make its mistakes.[83]

The idea of *kynde wit* remains of enormous importance to Langland throughout Piers Plowman. It is evidently a power for good, and so it remains even when Ymaginatif is setting it against *clergie* and grace. But in the last analysis, it is not sufficient of itself to produce salvation, even when it turns from a life orientated to the activities of this world to a much more contemplative mode. It stands condemned at the end of the poem by its separation from a *clergie* now seen to be crucial in the attempt to maintain a Christian society, but more categorically by the evident and absolute dependence of man on the activity of the divine. It is, I suspect, a sense of that dependence that leads Langland to portray the various crafts and the Cardinal Virtues as gifts of the Holy Ghost. This is, as we shall see, only one of the means by which Langland associates nature with the divine and thus both expresses and protects his sense of the critical importance of the natural in the pursuit of salvation.

---

[82] See also B XX 273–6.
[83] Conscience, we are told at B XX 150–1, is the one 'erthely creature' that Kynde will not 'at the laste' destroy.

## Chapter Two

# Kynde Knowynge

Like *kynde wit*, the idea of *kynde knowynge* recurs constantly in *Piers Plowman*.[1] Though several writers on the poem have stressed its importance, the critical literature exhibits considerable divergence over the understanding of the term.[2] As with *kynde wit*, *kynde* in *kynde knowynge* qualifies a word relating to cognition, and some critics have supposed *kynde wit* and *kynde knowynge* to be one and the same.[3] But whereas *kynde wit* often

---

[1] For a list of the occurrences of *kynde knowynge* and related terms see Sister M. A. Davlin, '*Kynde knowyng* as a Middle English equivalent for 'Wisdom' in *Piers Plowman* B', *MAE*, 50 (1981), 5–17, p. 15, n. 1. This piece and Sister Davlin's earlier article, '*Kynde Knowyng* as a Major Theme in *Piers Plowman* B', *RES* n.s. 22 (1971), 1–19, are highly important and influential treatments of the subject.

[2] Besides Davlin's articles see also Britton J. Harwood, 'Langland's *Kynde Knowyng* and the Quest for Christ', *MP*, 80 (1983), 242–55. Harwood sees *kynde knowynge* as equivalent to *notitia intuitiva*, intuitive knowledge, where the object of knowledge is immediately present to the knower (on this view see note 43 below). Harwood, p. 246, n. 25, provides a useful review of earlier definitions of *kynde knowynge*. The idea figures prominently in E. Vasta's *The Spiritual Basis of Piers Plowman* (The Hague, 1965), which attempts to read the poem as a description of the way to mystical union with God. *Kynde knowynge*, according to Vasta (p. 43), is a 'knowledge that is known immediately rather than mediately, that engages the affections as well as the intellect, and that is ultimately experiential'. For Vasta, Contemplation, the point at which the soul is deified, is a *kynde knowynge* of the Holy Spirit (p. 92). Vasta's stress on experience seems to me appropriate (though perhaps not for all *kynde knowynge*s; see below), but I do not accept the imposition of his mystical categories on *Piers Plowman*.

The idea of *kynde knowynge* does not seem very common in literature contemporary with *Piers Plowman*. There is an instance in *The Northern Homily Cycle*, ed. S. Nevanlinna, *Mémoires de la Société Néophilologique de Helsinki*, 38, 41 (1972, 1973) at line 8215: the *kind knawing* about God here seems, at least in part, to mean 'proper knowing', but the point of the passage is that possession of this knowledge is bound up with membership of the *kinde* of the Jews, and it is possible that this lies behind the choice of *kind* to qualify *knawing* and contributes to the meaning of that *kind*.

[3] For this view see Quirk (1953), p. 184 and Dunning (1937), p. 39; see also Erzgräber (1957), p. 45 and Hort (1938), pp. 69–81. E. D. Kirk, *The Dream Thought of Piers Plowman* (New Haven, 1972), pp. 37–8, n. 18 and Lawlor (1963), pp. 78, 99 speak of *kynde knowynge* in such a way as to appear to assimilate it to *kynde wit*. Frank (1957), p. 47, n. 1 and Vasta (1965), p. 43, n. 5 explicitly deny that the two terms are identical. I shall suggest that their relation to experience brings together the ideas of *kynde wit* and *kynde knowynge*, and Kynde Wit in A XII, closely associated with the good and reached through experience, looks as if it might be a form of *kynde knowynge*.

seems to be envisaged as something basic to man, this is not obviously the case with *kynde knowynge*, which Will frequently conceives himself as not having, and for which he makes several more or less frantic requests.[4] Perhaps more telling is one's sense that Will, in making these requests, cannot be particularly interested in having his knowledge through *kynde wit*; when he says to Studie

> . . . . youre man shal I worthe
> As longe as I lyve, bothe late and rathe,
> For to werche youre wille the while my lif dureth,
> With that ye kenne me kyndely to knowe what is Dowel.
>
> (B X 145–8)

it surely does not matter to him how his knowledge of Dowel comes about, as long as it does come. (The request itself indicates that Will does not conceive the knowing he asks for as something natural in the sense of innate, which certainly on occasion is a possible meaning for the *kynde* of *kynde wit*.) What Will seems to be concerned about is the quality of his knowledge. The same goes for Piers' remark that he knows Truth 'as kyndely as clerc doth hise bokes' (B V 538) – the point is that Piers knows Truth thoroughly and intimately; any suggestion that Piers' knowledge of Truth or *clercs'* knowledge of books came through natural faculties, for instance, would be awkward and irrelevant. In fact, the primary sense of *kynde* in *kynde knowynge*, whatever might be suggested through the polysemy of *kynde*, does not, I think, have to do with 'naturally available'. Indeed, it will be a question how much the term can be attached to any of the modern senses of nature.

In Middle English, *kynde* can mean 'proper', 'true', 'authentic' – 'as it really is', in fact, where the connection with 'nature' becomes apparent.[5] This meaning is evident on many occasions in *Piers Plowman*. The character Thought, we are told, called Will 'by my kynde name' (B VIII 72);[6] Christ

> loketh on us. . . .
> To knowen us by oure kynde herte. . . .
>
> (B XI 186–7)

---

[4] See B I 138, B VIII 111–12, B X 148, B XV 49; see also B XV 1–2.
[5] See MED under kind(e adj. 2. Davlin (1981), p. 10, remarks on this sense of *kynde*, connecting it with the meaning of the noun *kynde*, 'essential character'.
[6] Cf. A XI 254:

> Ne *mecaberis*, ne sle nouȝt, is the kynde englissh;

When Piers explains the Tree of Charity he refers to the *kynde* fruit *maidenhode* (B XVI 70–1). Langland may be making a point about the absolute naturalness of virginity (elsewhere, as we shall see in Chapter 4, he associates *kynde*ness with the motions of the flesh), but the force of *kynde* may simply be 'genuine' (as a mark of approbation) with *kynde* perhaps standing in opposition to *bastard* describing a lesser fruit in the previous line.

and those who advertise their charity in church windows are assured that

> God knoweth thi conscience and thi kynde wille[7], . . . .
>
> (B III 67)

Patience is qualified by *kynde* in the following:

> 'Lettrure and longe studie letteth fol monye,
> That they knoweth nat,' quod Concience, 'what is kynde Pacience. . . .'
>
> (C XV 181–2)

and there are several instances of love being called *kynde* where the 'true', 'proper', 'authentic' meaning seems very likely to be primary:

> Kynde love coveiteth noght no catel but speche.
>
> (B XIII 150)

> . . . *Caritas*, Kynde Loue an Engelysche[8], . . . .
>
> (C XIV 14)

I suggested in the last chapter that the meaning we are now considering is likely in the following passage, even though in the A version Langland wrote *kynde wit* rather than *kynde love* and was presumably thinking of that *wit* as naturally available:

> Ac kynde love shal come yit and Conscience togideres
> And make of lawe a laborer;
>
> (B III 299–300)

The adverb *kyndely* or *kyndeliche* can be used in a corresponding way:

> *Ergo* contricion, feith and conscience is kyndeliche Dowel, . . . .
>
> (B XIV 87)

Patience here professes to tell what Dowel *really* is.[9] We might gloss *kyndelyche* 'accurately', 'correctly' when we hear that 'þise newe clerkes' cannot 'construe kyndelyche þat poetes made' (C XVII 108–10), or when Peace asks

> Ho couthe kyndeliche with colour descreve
> Yf all þe world were whit or swan-whit all thynges?
>
> (C XX 213–4)

Similarly, in the following *kyndely* seems appropriately glossed 'properly':

> Thanne I courbed on my knees and cried hire of grace,
> And preide hire pitously to preye for my synnes,
> And also kenne me kyndely on Crist to bileve,
> That I myghte werchen His wille that wroghte me to man:
>
> (B I 79–82)

[7] Schmidt (1987), p. 26, glosses 'kynde wille' 'inner intention, real motives'.
[8] M. E. Goldsmith, *The Figure of Piers Plowman* (Cambridge, 1981), pp. 50, 58, relates this 'kynde love' to man's essential nature. In contrast Schroeder (1970), p. 26, considers the *kynde* to mark a limitation: *kynde* love is only *natural* love. Schmidt (1987), p. 151, glosses 'Kynde love' 'True affection'.
[9] Schmidt (1987), p. 166, glosses *kyndeliche* here 'essentially'.

What Will is asking for here is simply to be able to believe truly or properly in Christ. Any refinement as to the origin or specific character of that belief such as might be conveyed if we were to take *kyndely* as 'naturally' seems inappropriate.

Likewise, when Will asks to know something *kyndely* I think he is primarily asking for a proper knowledge of that thing. That this is the case is suggested by the use of 'wyte . . . witterly' as an equivalent of 'know . . . kyndely'. In the A version of the passage at B X 145–8 quoted above Will tells Studie

> . . . ȝour man shal I worþe
> For to werche ȝour wil [while] my lif duriþ,
> [To] kenne me kyndely to knowe what is dowel.

> (A XI 101–3)

A hundred and fifty lines later Will complains

> – ȝet am I neuere þe ner for nouȝt I haue walkid
> To wyte what is dowel witterly in herte, . . . .

> (A XI 258–9)

It looks as though Langland understands the *kyndely* of the first passage to mean very much the same as the *witterly* of the second. A similar interchange between *wyte* and *knowe* and *witterly* and *kyndeliche* occurs in the following C text passage. Peace is explaining the role of sin and suffering:

> For hadde they wist of no wo, wele hadde thay nat knowen;
> For no wiht woet what wele is þat neuere wo soffrede,
> Ne what is hoet hunger þat hadde neuere defaute.
> Ho couthe kyndeliche with colour descreue
> Yf all þe world were whit or swan-whit all thynges?
> Yf no nyht ne were, no man, y leue,
> Sholde ywyte witterly what day is to mene;
> Ne hadde god ysoffred of som oþer then hymsulue,
> He hadde nat wist witterly where deth were sour or swete.
> For sholde neuere riȝt riche man, þat lyueth in rest and in hele,
> Ywyte what wo is, ne were þe deth of kynde. . . .
>      Forthy god of his goednesse þe furste gom Adam
> Sette hym in solace furste and in souereyne merthe;
> And sethe he soffrede hym to synne, sorwe to fele,
> To wyte what wele was ther-thorw, kyndeliche to knowe.
> And aftur, god auntred hymsulue and toek Adames kynde
> To wyte what he hath soffred in thre sundry places,
> Bothe in heuene and in erthe – and now to helle he thenketh,
> To wyte what al wo is, þat woet of alle ioye.
>      *Omnia probate; quod bonum est tenete.*
> So hit shal fare bi this folk: here folye and here synne
> Shal lere hem what loue is and lisse withouten ende.
> For woet no wiht what werre is þer as pees regneth
> Ne what is witterliche wele til wel-a-way hym teche.

> (C XX 210–20, 227–38)

The equivalence of *knowe kyndeliche* and *wyte witterly* in this passage suggests that it might be unwise to put too much weight on meanings of *kynde* other than 'true', 'proper', 'authentic' when considering *kynde knowynge*, though this passage does itself offer certain possibilities, to which I shall return, for extending the meaning of *kynde knowynge* through word-play.

Much has been made of the plurality of meanings *kynde* possesses by Sister Mary Davlin in two very important and influential treatments of *kynde knowynge*.[10] She sees *kynde knowynge* as Langland's equivalent for 'wisdom'. The *kynde*, for her, is crucial:

> In *kynde*, with its wealth of 'natural' connotations, Langland found an array of interacting meanings perfectly though paradoxically suited to suggest the kind of knowledge called *gnosis* or *sapientia* in the Church tradition.[11]

Sister Davlin explains that this *sapientia* is a 'personal, loving experience of God'.[12] One of the authorities for the idea is St Paul:

> Paul teaches that the Christian, incorporated into Christ by baptism, has a co-naturality with him; through a deepening faith and love, he actually experiences Christ, his suffering and 'the power of his resurrection'.[13]

The polysemy of *kynde* permits *kynde knowynge* to cover various aspects of *sapientia* –

> experiential knowledge; intimate, loving knowledge; personal, thorough knowledge; knowledge as if by second nature; committed knowledge; connatural knowledge. Taken all together (as word play occasionally causes us to take them in *Piers Plowman*) these meanings become a descriptive definition of divine wisdom.[14]

The passages above come from Sister Davlin's second article on *kynde knowynge*, in which she concedes that 'the phrase in its various forms . . . obviously does not have the same meanings in its thirteen different occurrences'.[15] But in her first article she refers to '*kynde knowyng*, or wisdom'[16] and claims that

> By Passus v of the Visio, the meaning of *kynde knowyng* is established as a personal, loving, deep knowledge of Truth or Christ or God: in other words, as divine wisdom, *gnosis*, or *sapientia*.[17]

This determines her treatment of the uses of *kynde knowynge* later in the poem; she finds, for instance, that there is an ironic distance between Will's use of the term and what we know the term should really be used to mean.[18]

---

[10] See note 1 for details.
[11] Davlin (1981), p. 8.
[12] *Ibid.*, p. 7.
[13] *Ibid.*, p. 6.
[14] *Ibid.*, p. 15.
[15] *Ibid.*, p. 5.
[16] Davlin (1971), p. 1.
[17] *Ibid.*, p. 2.
[18] *Ibid.*, pp. 2–6.

But this view that *kynde knowynge* is established early in the poem as *sapientia* seems to me questionable. Take for instance Piers' claim in Passus B V to have a *kynde knowynge* of Truth:

> I knowe hym as kyndely as clerc doth hise bokes.
>
> (B V 538)

Piers' comparison implies that the *clerc* knows his books *kyndely*, but it is not at all clear that this *kynde knowynge* can be assimilated to Sister Davlin's definition. This clerkly knowing fails to fit that definition both as regards its object, since books are not Truth or Christ or God, and, one feels, as regards its character too: personal knowledge of God is surely not the same kind of knowledge as personal knowledge of books – the opposition Sister Davlin is suggesting between a theoretical knowledge of God and one that arises in an existential relationship with God as a person seems inapplicable in the case of a knowledge of books. And were we to apply the terms of Sister Davlin's later 'descriptive definition' of *sapientia* to knowledge of books we would be led into the plainly bizarre: however committed to their books scholars are, they do not become connatural with them.

This is to say that the objects of *kynde knowynge* may vary and that as they vary so may the character of the knowledge; there can be different kinds of 'proper' knowledge. Whilst knowledge of God to be 'proper' may indeed have to have the qualities Davlin suggests, it is not clear that this is so for a knowledge of books or sciences or crafts. These latter two are involved when Sister Davlin accuses Will of linguistic malpractice in speaking of *kynde knowynge*. Will has acknowledged to *Anima* his desire for universal knowledge:

> Alle the sciences under sonne and alle the sotile craftes
> I wolde I knewe and kouthe kyndely in myn herte!
>
> (B XV 48–9)

Sister Davlin characterises Will's wish as a desire for 'the detached, objective knowledge of the encyclopedist', 'a theoretical, loveless, irresponsible knowledge of "all things" '.[19] This is plainly nowhere near *kynde knowynge* as Sister Davlin understands it:

> It should not be called a *kynde knowyng* at all, though Will has so called it, because it is a perversion of both *kynde* and reason.[20]

But the reason given here shifts the grounds of the charge of linguistic incompetence. Sister Davlin refers to *Anima*'s rebuke of Will:

> 'Thanne artow inparfit,' quod he, 'and oon of Prides knyghtes!
> For swich a lust and likyng Lucifer fel from hevene:
> *Ponam pedem meum in aquilone et similis ero Altissimo.*
> 'It were ayeins kynde,' quod he, 'and alle kynnes reson
> That any creature sholde konne al, except Crist oone. . . .'
>
> (B XV 50–3)

---

[19] *Ibid.*, p. 5. On this see Harwood (1983), pp. 242–3.
[20] Davlin (1971), p. 5.

Langland is certainly picking up the *kyndely* of 'knewe and kouthe kyndely' in the *kynde* of 'ayeins kynde', but this is not enough to establish that it is illegitimate to speak of the knowledge Will requests as *kynde* in the sense of 'proper' or 'real' or 'thorough'. It makes perfect sense that thorough knowledge of all things in a created being should be deemed against the natural order, involving as it does the usurpation of the creator's omniscience by the creature.[21]

But the real reason for Sister Davlin's view that the knowledge Will desires is *unkynde* seems to be her perception of it as 'theoretical, loveless, and irresponsible'. One has to wonder, however, whether it is not appropriate that knowledge of sciences and crafts should be 'theoretical'. As for the 'loveless', surely Will's fervent desire gives evidence of some kind of love of the sciences and crafts, even if this may be 'irresponsible' love of knowledge for its own sake.[22] When Sister Davlin explains *kynde knowynge* as a loving knowledge of God, she has in mind a knowledge characterised by love of the object, but I suspect that the 'loveless' in her indictment of Will's desire to know all sciences and crafts *kyndely* does not relate to Will's attitude to these objects, but to Christian *caritas*, which love for sciences and crafts does not seem to involve – a pursuit of knowledge of 'all things' (Sister Davlin's inverted commas reveal her impatience with pursuit of this object) is not a pursuit of love of God and neighbour. One suspects that it is the unsatisfactoriness of the object that calls forth Sister Davlin's criticism, but if we accept that *kynde knowynge* can have objects such as books, and is not confined to God, her charge that Will is misusing the idea of *kynde knowynge* loses plausibility.

Sister Davlin is unhappy about Will's attitude when he calls for a *kynde knowynge* of Dowel. He is involved in 'theoretical theological disputes without love',[23] and his uses of *kynde knowynge* exhibit the influence of this improper involvement, since what he means by his requests is either 'Kindly tell me' or 'I want a thorough (though theoretical) knowledge' – he is not asking for the deep loving knowledge that is *sapientia*.[24] Again there is a difficulty over love: one will very likely not think of theological disputation as the centre of a life of loving commitment to God and neighbour – its poverty in these terms is perhaps revealed through the Doctor of Divinity at

[21] Coleman (1981), p. 137, takes Sister Davlin's line on this passage, but Vasta (1965), p. 46, supports the view I have expressed. *Anima* does not rebuke Will for an illegitimate use of words, or claim that the knowledge he desires is against *kynde*: what is wrong is the yearning for knowledge beyond one's station. The implication of *Anima*'s 'except Crist oone' is that Christ has precisely the *kynde knowynge* which Will requests, and this hardly suggests that the knowledge itself is suspect, as Sister Davlin's critique implies.

[22] It has been argued that Langland's God has a curiosity similar to man's own, which perhaps casts some doubt on this accusation of irresponsibility. See Jill Mann, 'Eating and Drinking in "Piers Plowman" ', *Essays and Studies*, n.s. 32 (1979). 26–43 (pp. 41f.).

[23] Davlin (1971), p. 3.

[24] *Ibid.*, p. 3.

Conscience's feast in B XIII – but Will's unremitting pursuit of Dowel and his anguish at his failure to find it point both to a passionate commitment to Dowel, and to the fact that his interest is by no means only theoretical, or 'passive', as Sister Davlin styles it;[25] rather it is of profound existential significance to him. His attempt to lay hold upon Dowel through intercourse with figures from the life of the intellect turns out to be misguided, but it is not certain that Will is to be blamed for this. The approach he adopts, 'theoretical' only in that it involves intellectual disputation, not because Will is uncommitted to it, can be argued to proceed from the failure of Kynde Wit and the life of honest labour it sponsored as the centre of an understanding of the life of virtue. The poem, taking Will with it, turns to the life of the intellect in the hope that answers can be found there. It is not only Will, apparently, who believes in the pursuit of a *kynde knowynge* of Dowel through the life of the intellect, for Studie answers Will's request for it with

> Tel Clergie thise tokenes, and to Scripture after,
> To counseille thee kyndely to knowe what is Dowel.

(B X 216–7)

I doubt Langland is asking us, as we read this, to see Studie's use of the idea of *kynde knowynge* as superficial.[26]

Sister Davlin's treatment of *kynde knowynge* is thoroughly conditioned by her referring instances of the term back to the notion of *sapientia*, which she takes the early occurrences of *kynde knowynge* to establish as the essential meaning of the term. But this practice seems dubious, since the objects of *kynde knowynge* differ, and it is possible that the character of the knowledge differs accordingly. It may be that, for some objects, a 'theoretical', rather than a personally engaged knowledge is entirely authentic: it is a mistake to appropriate into the very meaning of *kynde* the properties of a particular sort of *kynde knowynge*, such as Piers has of Truth, for instance (when much of what Sister Davlin sees as essential to *kynde knowynge* as a whole does seem to be evident in the particular instance).

This question of the object is critical: it is wrong to suppose that a mention of *kynde knowynge* includes reference to the object of knowledge, as the equation with *gnosis* or *sapientia* suggests. In most cases in *Piers Plowman* *kynde knowynge* does not occur without further specification of its object or effect. *Kynde knowynge* is, in fact, not a single entity, but a manner of knowing various things. And one is not obliged to suppose that all the connotations of *kynde* are in play whenever *kynde knowynge* of whatever object is mentioned.

---

[25] *Ibid.*, p. 6.
[26] Though in the light of the poem's later insistence on the importance of experience one might come to have reservations about the idea that a *kynde knowynge* of Dowel can be arrived at through Clergie and Scripture on their own. See note 45.

As we have seen, the apparent interchangeability of to *knowe kyndely* and to *wyte witterly* suggests that connotations deriving from the polysemy of *kynde* are not central to the meaning of *kynde knowynge*: it would be possible for the term to mean simply 'thorough knowledge'. But Langland's acknowledged propensity for word-play demands that we should be alive to the possibility that other meanings are operative in some of the instances of *kynde knowynge*; we must, however, not force interpretation so as to foist those meanings onto instances in which they seem only dubiously applicable.

Though Sister Davlin's earlier unqualified identification of *kynde knowynge* and wisdom seems questionable, her later suggestions as to how the various meanings of *kynde* might be functioning in the phrase *kynde knowynge* are well worth pursuing, and the possibility that *kynde knowynge* might indeed on occasion be an equivalent for *sapientia* is not ruled out by a demonstration that it cannot always be so. The case for the identification is strongest in the earlier instances of *kynde knowynge*, but the use of the idea in Holy Church's speech is problematic to a degree, and I want to reserve discussion of this passage till later.

Among the connotations of *kynde* which Sister Davlin finds relevant for *kynde knowynge* is 'loving'. With this there is no difficulty. The connotation is certainly not inappropriate to Will's request that he should be taught to know Dowel *kyndely*. Will's intense commitment to the search for Dowel can, as I have already suggested, be taken as evidence of his love of it. There is no reason to suppose either that the knowledge of sciences and crafts should not be loving. When we are told of the *kynde wit*ted sages that

alle hir kynde knowying com but of diverse sightes

(B XII 136)

we are at liberty to suppose that these inferior insights were cherished so devotedly as to justify the term 'loving knowledge'; though, equally, we might feel that there is no real pressure to mobilise this connotation of *kynde* in this instance. Sister Davlin is thinking in terms of a knowledge of persons when she finds this connotation significant, and that is the case too with her suggestion that *kynde knowynge* can mean personal knowledge ('personal' seems to amplify both the authenticity and the lovingness of the knowledge: it is not in its own right a possible meaning of *kynde*).

The meaning 'as if by second nature' often seems plausible. In fact, perhaps to say that some piece of knowledge is 'second nature', need not be to say much more than that it is thoroughly known. But a stricter understanding of the phrase may be thought appropriate in relation to Langland's *kynde knowynge*. We have seen that Will asks to know all sciences and crafts 'kyndely in herte', and this is not the only occasion on which *kynde knowynge* and the heart are connected.[27] The heart is said to be the par-

[27] See also B I 142, 165.

ticular dwelling place of *Anima* (B IX 55–6), and this being so, one might well suppose that the nature of the individual resides particularly in the heart, and that knowledge in the heart has been so deeply internalised as to become 'second nature'. Piers compares his *kynde* knowledge of Truth to the knowledge clerks have of books (B V 538). As well as claiming proper knowledge, Piers may be suggesting that knowledge of Truth is as natural to him as knowledge of books is to scholars – perhaps this is more than 'second nature'; the nature of clerks is constituted by their involvement with books, and Piers may be claiming that his nature is similarly deeply conditioned by his relationship with Truth. Piers' journey to Truth ends with the awareness of Truth dwelling in one's heart (B V 605ff.),[28] and here one might appropriately speak both of knowledge that conditions the nature and co-naturality of knower and known: with Truth in the heart one might well be supposed to become Truth in some sense.

Holy Church locates the *kynde knowynge* of which she speaks in the heart, thus pointing to its depth and intimacy, and liberating the suggestions in *kynde* of a relation to the inner nature of the knower.[29] But this may not exhaust the meaning of *kynde knowynge*. The passage is very difficult and a close examination is required. Holy Church has been discoursing on Truth for Will's benefit:

> 'Whan alle tresors arn tried, Truthe is the beste.
> Lereth it th[u]s lewed men, for lettred it knoweth –
> That Treuthe is tresor the trieste on erthe.'
>     'Yet have I no kynde knowynge,' quod I, 'ye mote kenne me bettre
> By what craft in my cors it comseth, and where.'
>     'Thow doted daffe!' quod she, 'dulle are thi wittes.
> To litel Latyn thow lernedest, leode, in thi youthe:
> *Heu michi quia sterilem duxi vitam iuvenilem!*
> It is a kynde knowynge that kenneth in thyn herte
> For to loven thi Lord levere than thiselve,
> No dedly synne to do, deye theigh thow sholdest –
> This I trowe be truthe; who kan teche thee bettre,
> Loke thow suffre hym to seye, and sithen lere it after;
> For thus witnesseth his word; worche thow therafter.

(B I 135–47)

The first *kynde knowynge* is glossed 'natural knowledge' by Schmidt and 'natural understanding' by Pearsall. Schmidt takes it as a *kynde knowynge* of

---

[28] Vasta (1965), pp. 107–8, understands this passage to describe the achievement of that unitive life which is the goal of mystical endeavour: it would certainly be appropriate to recall Holy Church's remark that the true man is 'a god by the Gospel' (B I 90).

[29] Vasta (1965), p. 43, sees the *kynde knowynge* of which Holy Church speaks as affective and not merely intellectual. The whole poem can be seen in terms of a progression from intellectual to affective knowledge. See Lawlor (1962), and James Simpson, 'From Reason to Affective Knowledge: Modes of Thought and Poetic Form in *Piers Plowman*', *MAE*, 55 (1986), 1–23. Simpson, pp. 14–15, relates affective knowledge to *kynde knowynge*, speaking of 'a sapiential, experiential, "kynde" knowledge of God'.

Truth,[30] but for Pearsall it appears to be free standing; he suggests that 'the concept [*kynde knowynge*] holds a position between' Kynde Wit and Reason.[31] However, Holy Church's conclusion, 'This I trowe be truthe; who kan teche thee bettre, . . .' seems to pick up Will's request that she should *kenne* him *bettre* and so suggest that the 'it' in the second line of Will's response refers to Truth, in which case the mention of *kynde knowynge* will seem irrelevant unless it is a *kynde knowynge* which relates to Truth.

There now arises the issue of how to gloss *kynde*. It would be possible to understand Will's remark as follows: 'But I have no natural knowledge (relating to Truth) and therefore you must inform me better . . .'. Here, though, the mention of *natural* knowledge seems slightly curious, since Will could be expected to say simply that he had insufficient knowledge without bothering to refer to the source from which that knowledge derived. These expectations would be fulfilled if *kynde* were glossed 'proper', and, especially if 'Yet' is taken as 'still' and Will's remark understood to be a complaint that Holy Church's discourse on Truth has not delivered what might have been expected of it, this interpretation perhaps has the added advantage of avoiding a sense of hiatus when *kynde knowynge* is not further defined when Will makes reference to it. We would not need further definition if we are being told that, in spite of all Holy Church has said, Will has no really satisfying knowledge. The slight oddness and awkwardness of 'natural knowledge' could be explained as the price to be paid for having Will fall into the absurdity of claiming not to have something he in fact possesses (this on one possible understanding of the second *kynde knowynge*), but, judging, for the moment, simply on the run of the passage for each alternative, the gloss 'proper' seems to me to be marginally preferable. I think that, just as sixty lines earlier, when he asks Holy Church that she should 'kenne [him] kyndely on Crist to bileve', he is concerned to be given a proper belief in Christ, so here Will is still confronting the inadequacy of his spiritual equipment, and the *kynde* term still has reference to properness and authenticity.

If the first *kynde knowynge* does mean proper knowledge, this still does not establish the meaning of *kynde knowynge* in Holy Church's reply to Will, though I think it makes the sense 'natural knowledge' more difficult. A crux in the interpretation of this passage is the 'It' in 'It is a kynde knowynge . . .'. It might be that Holy Church is countering Will's claim that he has no *kynde knowynge* of Truth. She might be saying in effect, 'What *kens* love of God and avoidance of deadly sin within you *is* a *kynde knowynge*'. In this interpretation, Holy Church would be affirming the existence already within Will of a *kynde knowynge*, so that we could easily understand *kynde* as 'natural'. One can then understand what the *kynde*

---

[30] Schmidt (1987), on B I 139, p. 14. See also, e.g., Stokes (1984), p. 84.
[31] Pearsall (1978), on C I 136, p. 49.

*knowynge kens* as truth – 'This (i.e. love of God and avoidance of deadly sin) I trowe be truthe.' And this notion of a natural knowledge of truth may be aligned with the scholastic notion of *synderesis*, the natural and inalienable attachment all men possess to the sovereign good.[32] Furthermore, the definition of Truth this interpretation yields is well accommodated to the immediate context, in which Truth and Love are very closely approximated, perhaps made identical.[33]

But there is another way of understanding the passage. One might take the 'It' of 'It is a kynde knowynge. . . .' to refer to Truth. This will mean that this 'It' and the 'it' regarding which Will demands further clarification will refer to the same thing. This would, perhaps, make things easier for the reader than having the referents different. The 'This' of Holy Church's conclusion at line 145 will then embrace the whole contents of lines 142 to 144, which is rather crisper than having it cover only what the *kynde knowynge kens*,[34] and Truth would be the knowledge that one is to love God and do no deadly sin.

To understand Truth in this way might be thought to involve too high a claim for a piece of knowledge which is, after all, common to all Christians, perhaps to all men. But the *kynde* is crucial. It carries with it, I think, the guarantee that knowledge will issue in practice, a practice which conforms to the will of God. This justifies naming the source of that practice Truth, which is also a name for God. The practice is Love, and such a relation between Truth and Love, in no way belittling to Truth, – in fact according it priority – might lie behind Langland's use of both Truth and Love in Holy Church's speech and his insistence on Truth rather than the perhaps more obvious Love as the best treasure. If one can appropriate Truth, Love will follow.[35]

This suggestion concerning the practice of Love arising out of the *kynde knowynge* that is Truth has its grounds in lines in Holy Church's speech which occur shortly after those just discussed. Holy Church has just explained how Truth tells that love is 'triacle of hevene' (B I 148–58):

> Forthi is love ledere of the Lordes folke of hevene,
> And a meene, as the mair is, [inmiddes] the kyng and the commune;
> Right so is love a ledere and the lawe shapeth:
> Upon man for hise mysdedes the mercyment he taxeth.

---

[32] See Chapter 1, note 7.

[33] See J. A. W. Bennett, ed., *Piers Plowman: The Prologue and Passus I–VII of the B text* (Oxford, 1972), on B I 140 (Schmidt 142), p. 112.

[34] Some degree of hesitation might precede an understanding of exactly what 'This' referred to with the smaller coverage: would it be the avoidance of deadly sin, one might wonder, before realising that it would include also love of God.

[35] We might also note that to have Truth a *kynde knowynge* does justice to Truth's propositional aspect.

## Kynde Knowynge

And for to knowen it kyndely – it comseth by myght,
And in the herte, there is the heed and the heighe welle.
For in kynde knowynge in herte ther [coms]eth a myght –
And that falleth to the Fader that formed us alle,
Loked on us with love and leet his sone dye
Mekely for oure mysdedes, to amenden us alle.

(B I 159–68)

This is another very difficult passage. The first difficulty arises over the knowing of love *kyndely* in line 163. It has been supposed that Holy Church is saying that a *kynde knowynge* of love comes about by *myght*.[36] But the 'it' of 'it comseth by myght' seems awkward in this case, and the relation of the statement made to the explanation offered in line 165 is by no means clear. I think that with 'it comseth . . .' Holy Church supplies the *kynde knowynge* of love which she says she is going to give in 'and for to knowen it kyndely'. The second difficulty is over how to take the *myghts*. Several critics have supposed the first to refer to the power of God and the second to a capacity arising within man.[37] Besides the fact that understanding *myght* as divine power seems somewhat arbitrary, this surely involves a rather difficult shift in the meaning of *myght*. I would prefer to understand the two *myghts* as referring to the same thing, which I understand to be a spiritual capacity or energy. Holy Church is saying that love arises out of a spiritual capacity which is itself generated by a *kynde knowynge* in the heart. This explains why 'the heed and the heighe welle' of love is in the heart. Holy Church is, I think, stating a general rule to the effect that *kynde* knowledge produces spiritual energies within the individual. In the case of love it is the *kynde*ness of the knowledge that one should love that engenders within one the power so to do. The *kynde* knowledge produces the practice. This is a fact of our nature for which God is responsible, and which demonstrates the love God had for us in creation, a love which is continued in the sending of His son for our salvation. The treasure of Truth can be understood as that *kynde knowynge* which brings with it the power to love. When Piers speaks of Truth dwelling in the heart in a chain of charity (B V 606–7), we could understand him to be speaking of the presence of the *kynde knowynge* that teaches charity, which is accordingly also brought about in the heart, and which, reciprocally, guarantees the presence of Truth.

In the passages just discussed, it seems to me that the first references to *kynde knowynge* are in each case better taken as 'proper knowledge' than as 'natural knowledge'. This would exert a degree of pressure in favour of 'proper knowledge' as the meaning throughout the passages, since word-play in this situation might very well appear to the poet irresponsible and

[36] Davlin (1981), pp. 11–12.
[37] So Davlin (1981), pp. 11–12. See also Bennett (1972), on B I 161 (Schmidt 163); Schmidt (1987), on B I 163, 165, p. 15; Pearsall (1978), on C I 159–60, p. 51.

merely bewildering rather than enlightening.[38] But the pressure, even given complete certainty on the meaning of the first *kynde knowynge*s, would not be absolutely compelling. Considerations external to the passages seem to me more likely to resolve the issue between 'proper' and 'natural'.

I want, therefore, to consider whether or not the context of the poem as a whole supports the meaning 'natural' in these passages, taking 'natural' in the senses in which it relates to the natural capacities and condition of man. Firstly, what of the possibility of understanding the *kynde knowynge* that either is Truth or teaches Truth as an innate capacity?[39] Truth is presented in *Piers Plowman* as something to be sought after; Piers details the stages of a journey towards it, and people go on pilgrimage to reach it. If Truth is an innate knowledge, the sense of Truth as something difficult of attainment is betrayed. And Truth can hardly be the best treasure in the pursuit of salvation if men possess it innately, for, vital though Truth may be, whether individuals will be saved or damned will depend on something else. If, on the other hand, we were to think in terms of an innate knowledge *of* Truth, we could understand this knowledge to inform one that one must be true, and this would not imply that Truth was already possessed at the outset. Nevertheless, it might seem rather awkward to describe a universal innate knowledge of Truth in the same terms as the evidently very privileged and apparently uninnate knowledge of Truth that Piers possesses and towards which all men are to strive: for Piers seems to envisage knowing Truth *kyndely* as the end point of a journey (B V 537ff.).

Again, we might try to interpret *kynde knowynge* in terms of natural capacities, so that Truth, or a knowledge of it, would be naturally acquired.[40] But to speak in these terms of the best treasure man can acquire, that which gives him salvation, would seem to be utterly Pelagian. Piers, as we have seen, lays himself open to this charge in making the claims he does for *kynde wit*, but he still very clearly acknowledges the need for grace. And if we return to the particular context, we can ask why knowledge acquired through natural capacities in particular should give rise to a *myght*. As a final consideration one might note that *kynde knowynge* frequently has as its

---

[38] Except, perhaps, if Holy Church is taken to be confuting Will's claim not to have *kynde knowynge*, in which case the attention would be fixed specifically on the concept of *kynde knowynge*, and investigation of exactly how it is *kynde* might appropriately be invited.

[39] Several critics have seen the idea of *synderesis* behind Langland's *kynde knowynge*. See Pearsall (1978), on C 1 141–2, p. 50; Hort (1938), pp. 80–1; Dunning (1980), p. 26 (and also Dunning (1937), p. 53); Harwood (1983), p. 250. Other writers who apparently consider *kynde knowynge* something innate include Bloomfield (1961), pp. 25, 111, 152–3 and Lawlor (1962), pp. 40–1.

[40] See Coleman (1981), pp. 45ff. Vasta (1965), p. 86, relates *kynde knowynge* to a natural capacity in man to love God, a natural desire to possess him and a natural inclination to lead the moral life. The *kynde knowynge* is not innate, but acquired by natural means on the basis of these capacities.

central denotation 'proper knowledge', and wonder whether entities should be multiplied; the meaning 'proper knowledge' seems to fit in all cases. Though Langland is deeply alive to the possibility of words bearing more than one meaning, doubts may legitimately be felt as to whether he would be so cavalier in shifting about the meaning of what is clearly a very important term.

*Kynde knowynge* as we have discussed it so far offers only very precarious support for any conviction regarding the goodness of the natural. The meaning of *kynde* in *kynde knowynge* seems likely to be too distinct from the idea of natural in the required senses to offer Langland any very solid support for this position. Nevertheless, it is possible to discern an attachment of *kynde knowynge* to the basic conditions of man's life. Sister Davlin suggested that *kynde knowynge* at its fullest would involve experiential knowledge. She took 'experiential' to be a possible meaning of *kynde*, and this seems to me doubtful,[41] but experience does seem to be involved in certain important kinds of 'proper' knowledge. In these cases *kynde knowynge* may not mean experiential knowledge, but experience is required if the knowledge is indeed to be proper. 'Experience' here is not to be understood solely as experience of the object of knowledge (which is, I take it, what Sister Davlin has in mind when she speaks of experiential knowledge). There *are* claims that a thing is not known unless experienced, but Langland also argues that experience of a thing is inadequate to bring proper knowledge without experience of its opposite. There are suggestions too that experience of life in general, and in particular an exposure to the suffering that flesh is heir to, is productive of proper and important knowledge.[42] This may be the case in the following lines, though I think it is possible to understand them otherwise. Will perhaps proposes for himself a course in general experience of life when he tells the Friars who have spoken to him on the subject of Dowel:

> 'I have no kynde knowyng,' quod I, 'to conceyve alle thi wordes,
>   Ac if I may lyve and loke, I shal go lerne bettre.'

(B VIII 58–9)

Will is saying that he has no proper knowledge through which to get a firm grasp of what the Friars are saying, and may well be suggesting that he might acquire that *kynde knowynge* if he is permitted to go on experiencing.

But the connection of *kynde knowynge* with experience is clearer in the following passage. Having established above through the C version the

---

[41] The MED entry kind(e adj. does not offer support for Davlin's suggestion.
[42] A. V. C. Schmidt, 'The Inner Dreams of *Piers Plowman*', *MAE*, 55 (1986), 24–40 points to a conviction on Langland's part of the importance of suffering for the acquisition of spiritual insight (pp. 36–7).

equivalence of to *knowe kyndely* and to *wyte witterly* I give the passage here
as it appears in B:

> For no wight woot what wele is, that nevere wo suffrede,
> Ne what is hoot hunger, that hadde nevere defaute.
> If no nyght ne weere, no man, as I leve,
> Sholde wite witterly what day is to meene.
> Sholde nevere right riche man that lyveth in reste and ese
> Wite what wo is, ne were the deeth of kynde.
> So God that bigan al of his goode wille
> Bicam man of a mayde mankynde to save,
> And suffrede to be sold, to se the sorwe of deying,
> The which unknytteth alle care, and comsynge is of reste.
> For til *modicum* mete with us, I may it wel avowe,
> Woot no wight, as I wene, what is ynogh to mene.
> Forthi God, of his goodnesse, the firste gome Adam,
> Sette hym in solace and in sovereyn murthe;
> And siththe he suffred hym synne, sorwe to feele –
> To wite what wele was, kyndeliche to know it.
> And after, God auntrede hymself and took Adames kynde
> To wite what he hath suffred in thre sondry places,
> Bothe in hevene and in erthe – and now til helle he thenketh,
> To wite what alle wo is, that woot of alle joye.[43]
> So it shal fare by this folk: hir folie and hir synne
> Shal lere hem what langour is, and lisse withouten ende.
> Woot no wight what werre is ther that pees regneth,
> Ne what is witterly wele til "weylawey" hym teche.

(B XVIII 205–28)

Experience of *defaute* is required here to know properly what hunger is, and
further, the *defaute* implied in *modicum* is essential for proper knowledge of
*ynowe*. By itself, experience of *wele* is insufficient to give one proper knowl-
edge of *wele*, and this provides a vindication for the experiences of suffering
and of death, that form of suffering against which it is impossible to protect
oneself. The phrase 'deeth *of kynde*' (why the reference to *kynde*?, one
asks) suggests that Langland is thinking in terms of a vindication of the
natural order. The natural order with all its suffering and its sin can be seen
as positive because of the positive role played by death, the ultimate suffer-
ing and the reward of sin; for death guarantees proper knowledge, which is
here also, it now appears, natural knowledge because it derives from the
realm of *kynde*. The realm of *kynde* contains the essential experience, and if
it had seemed that that realm was condemned by the presence of suffering
and death, this turns out to be very much not the case. The mention of the

---

[43] This passage seems to me to put considerable pressure on Harwood's (1983) identification of
*kynde knowynge* with *notitia intuitiva*, where the object of knowledge is immediately present to
the knower. *Wele* was surely immediately present to Adam in Paradise, and yet he apparently
did not know it *kyndely*.

good will of God who 'bigan al' just after the remark about the 'deeth of kynde' is further assurance of the beneficence of the natural order and the threatening death. Man needs suffering because *wo* is the condition of a true appreciation of *wele*, as is hinted, perhaps, in the assonance between *wele* and *weylawey*, and the very matter-of-fact coupling of *langour* and *lisse*.

If man needs experience of evil to know *wele*, so does God. That, at least, seems to be what is suggested, though the more obvious point of concentration is God's knowledge of *wo*. God's need involves him in the assumption of man's *kynde* and exposure to the *kynde* course of man's life. (These senses of *kynde* enrich the *kyndeliche* in 'kyndeliche to knowe' in line 220.) This constitutes a powerful vindication of the natural condition of man, which is shown to be bound up with the competence of God to be fully God, since for a true knowledge and appreciation of the joy he is said already to know, God, like the rich man, needs to suffer. The C text follows its claim that God has gone to find out about *wo*, knowing already about *ioye*, with the text *Omnia probate; quod bonum est tenete.* In this context one might take the relation between experiencing everything and the good as one of condition and fulfilment, such that only when God has experienced everything, including suffering, can he really *bonum tenere*, in the sense both of truly apprehending *wele* and of preserving perfection flawless.

The *omnia probate* here takes us back to Kynde Wit in A XII which was reached in the company of *omnia probate*. *Omnia probate* was there described as a 'pore thing', and the present passage suggests that this might be because of its association with suffering (we recall Will's exposure to disease and death at the end of A XII). However that may be, in experience we can see a convergence of *kynde wit* and *kynde knowynge*. Experience of the natural course of life can lead to a wisdom designated 'natural', but, as we have just seen, this experience can give proper knowledge of *wele*. God's knowledge of *wele* is not only proper, but also natural in that it arises from exposure to the natural course of life, through an adoption of the nature of man.

We might say that *kynde wit* in this sense, *wit* attained through natural experience, is a condition of *kynde knowynge*. I think this may be the case for more than proper knowledge of *wo* and *wele*. At the end of the poem, Will suffers exposure to Elde, who visits him with various physical incapacities. Ultimately responsible for this is the figure Kynde, God the Creator of the natural realm, now considered in his character as destroyer, as the natural forces over which he presides bring mankind, and Will in particular, towards the grave:

> And as I seet in this sorwe, I saugh how Kynde passede,
> And deeth drogh neigh me – for drede gan I quake,
> And cryde to Kynde, 'Out of care me brynge!

Lo! how Elde the hoore hath me biseye:
Awreke me if youre wille be, for I wolde ben hennes!'
   'If thow wolt be wroken, wend into Unitee,
And hold thee there evere, til I sende for thee;
And loke thow konne som craft er thow come thennes.'
      'Counseille me, Kynde,' quod I, 'what craft be best to lerne?'
      'Lerne to love,' quod Kynde, 'and leef alle othere.'
      'How shal I come to catel so, to clothe me and feede?'
      'And thow love lelly, lakke shal thee nevere
Weede ne worldly mete, while thi lif lasteth.'
   And there by conseil of Kynde I comsed to rome
Thorugh Contricion and Confession til I cam to Unite.

(B XX 199–213)

The name of the instructor perhaps hints that this instruction is to be regarded as *kynde*. It is so in various ways. What the Dreamer is told by Kynde could be considered *kynde wit* because it seems to be the result of exposure to natural sufferings endemic to the experience of life. We may refer again to Kynde Wit in Passus A XII. But we should also, I think, regard the knowledge Will is offered here as authentic – it is a *kynde knowynge*, which could perhaps be identified with Sister Davlin's *sapientia*, and with Truth, if that is indeed earlier defined as a *kynde knowynge* instructing one to love.[44] We may feel too that here at last Will's quest for Dowel ends; here he knows it *kyndely* as the practice of Love. The authenticity of the teaching is evidenced by the fact that it is delivered by God *in propria persona* – this is the only time in the poem when God addresses Will directly. The lesson carries complete authority, an authority demonstrated by the compelling force it bears for Will; no argument this time, but an immediately undertaken journey to Unity. Perhaps it is because Will is now, as he has not always been, actually suffering, evidently deeply immersed in the flow of natural experience, rather than merely looking on, that the lesson which presents itself carries conviction – it has been learnt on the pulses.[45] The sense of authenticity, indeed that we have here the quintessence of wisdom, is reinforced by the emergence of the teaching *ex extremis*, out of Will's confrontation with death, by the absoluteness of the teaching – 'alle othere' is to be left, by its occurrence at the end of Will's life and by its bringing his long journey to its conclusion in Unity.

[44] Frank (1957), p. .47, suggests that Will's request for *kynde knowynge* is met when the poem turns to Charity, there being no more explicit requests for *kynde knowynge* after Passus B XV. See also Kirk (1972), p. 191. Vasta (1965), however, supposes (p. 125) that Will achieves the *kynde knowynge* of which Holy Church speaks in his vision of the Passion and Harrowing of Hell. But Davlin (1971), pp. 16–17, sees the meeting with Kynde in B XX as the culmination of Will's search for *kynde knowynge*.

[45] See Schmidt (1986), pp. 33, 36–7. In view of the connection between *kynde knowynge* of significant things and experience, one wonders what to make of Studie's claim that Clergie and Scripture will be able to give Will a *kynde knowynge* of Dowel; the need for experience may contribute to Conscience's decision to leave Clergie and set out with Patience (B XIII 179ff.). See note 26.

Here, then, is a triumphant vindication of the *kynde knowynge* derived from experience and of the natural course of life which generates that experience. The experience of life itself, with all the weight of the destructive indignities to which it subjects man, turns out not only to be necessary for a full appreciation of the bliss of heaven (for God as well as man, it seems), but to be a most effective instrument, perhaps indeed *the* most effective, for urging man towards his salvation.

## Chapter Three

# *Kynde as God*

I have suggested that Langland wished to display the *kynde* as a force for good, and perhaps the most striking expression of this desire is his personification of God as Kynde. Though in its origins and impact his figure may owe debts (which I shall explore) to other medieval Natures, Langland's identification of God as Kynde sets his Nature figure at a considerable remove from those other Natures. It also seems to me to involve Langland in an examination of the problem of evil: his identification seems to insist upon the rightness of the natural realm since it makes God directly responsible for it, and yet from certain perspectives that realm is plainly disastrous. How can the appearances of Kynde's dispensation be reconciled with what must be the reality of his love? The difficulty may become evident to Langland only after he has created his God called Kynde. Certainly, an initially untroubled treatment of Kynde is succeeded by presentations in which the problematic aspects of Kynde's disposition of his realm are made increasingly apparent (we might be reminded of what happens to *kynde wit* in the course of the poem). But, as he confronts the problem of evil, Langland's sense of the goodness of the natural order which Kynde superintends does not disappear but deepens. The evil in Kynde's dispensation is recognised and exposure to it eventually understood, in ways we have already begun to explore, to be spiritually productive. Indeed, such exposure may be more beneficial for man's spiritual life than more orthodox kinds of instruction: Will seems to derive more assistance from his suffering under Kynde's destructive power at the end of the poem than he does from hearing about Kynde from Wit in Passus B IX or contemplating his activity in the *Myddelerthe* vision of Passus B XI. Langland is, I think, optimistically insisting on the accommodatedness even of the fallen world of sin and suffering to the spiritual aspirations of man.

It may be suggested that through his exploration of Kynde Langland reaches a fuller understanding of man's fallenness. The clarity of the attitude to sin expressed in the text of Truth's pardon seems no longer altogether appropriate when sin can be understood as having a positive purpose in the divine scheme of things. It may in part be because he feels that the figure Kynde provides a more accurate focus on the nature of sin than does Truth that Langland permits the virtual replacement of Truth by Kynde as the poem's designation of God the Father. Exactly what motivated the movement from Truth to Kynde is perhaps inevitably undiscernable among the various possibilities to which the semantic fecundity of *kynde* gives rise. But what I shall be pointing to is a number of optimistic suggestions about the nature of God and man and the relationship between the human and the divine that the adoption of Kynde as a name for God puts before us.

I have taken it for granted that Langland's Kynde is God. A reading of the commentators might suggest otherwise: we find Kynde understood as an agent of God and taken as a female figure (and therefore presumably not as God the Father).[1] But there is little room for uncertainty on this point – Langland's figure is identified quite explicitly as the Father Creator:

> 'Kynde,' quod Wit, 'is creatour of alle kynnes thynges,
> Fader and formour of al that evere was maked –
> And that is the grete God that gynnyng hadde nevere,
> Lord of lif and of light, of lisse and of peyne.

(B IX 26–9)

The C text here perhaps goes even further in making clear that Kynde is the Christian Creator in identifying Kynde as love and everlasting life:

> . . . .Kynde, that alle kyne thynges wrouhte,
> The which is loue and lyf þat last withouten ende.

(C X 168–9)

(We shall find Langland repeatedly associating his Kynde with love, and it seems probable that suggestions of love and benevolence attach to the figure in virtue of the meaning of *kynde*.)[2] At B XI 325 Kynde is again designated *creatour*. These identifications determine the sense of Kynde in two of the three sequences in the poem in which Kynde is a major figure. There is no reason to suppose that in the third sequence in B XX Kynde represents anything else, though here the power over the world which Kynde possesses by virtue of being the world's creator expresses itself in ways not self-evidently creative.

One possible reason for the confusion of commentators in this area is the strangeness of Langland's identification. The Chartrian tradition offers a female Nature figure, a 'goddess' who superintends creative processes in

---

[1] Joseph A. Longo, '*Piers Plowman* and the Tropological Matrix: Passus XI and XII', *Anglia*, 82 (1964), 291–308, takes Kynde to be an agent of God (p. 299). Several critics refer to Kynde as female; See Lawlor (1962), p. 116, Robertson and Huppé (1951), p. 230, and M. W. Bloomfield, *Piers Plowman as a Fourteenth Century Apocalypse* (New Brunswick, 1961), pp. 143–4, where curious shifts in the gender of the possessives referring to Kynde are to be found.

[2] See discussion in the following chapter.

subordination to God, but Langland's identification of the personified Nature as God is unparalleled in prior literary texts. Critics betray a desire to see Langland's personification as another instance of the *vicaria Dei* figure, but the passages from *Piers Plowman* I have cited will not bear such an interpretation. From where, then, might Langland's figure be derived?

Edgar Knowlton, who pioneered the study of Nature in medieval literature, recognised how Langland's Kynde stood apart from other medieval Nature figures:

> In the mind of the alliterative poet, Nature, or Kuynde, is not a feminine power subordinate to God, but is God Himself, in accordance with a definition to which some of the early Church Fathers objected, a definition like the Stoic equations.[3]

But Knowlton does not level a charge of heretical pantheism (to which the Stoic conception is open) at Langland's figure, finding it to be connected with 'theological powers and the appropriate domain of the soul'.[4] He thinks that 'By metonomy, Kind is substituted for the God of Kind'.[5]

Though he points to the similarity between Stoic and early Christian definitions of God and Langland's Kynde, Knowlton does not make it clear whether he thinks the creation of Langland's figure was influenced by such definitions. The process of metonymy he proposes does not require any knowledge of prior identifications of God and Nature, though these might provide an author with a suggestion and some supportive precedents. The idea that Langland's figure is pantheistic is rightly rejected,[6] but this leaves us with no very satisfactory answer to the question as to where Langland derived his conception from – we could at best say that Langland's metonymy, through which he arrives at a very different conception, was nevertheless prompted by the Stoic definitions to which Knowlton refers.[7]

Such, of course, might be the case. Langland's perhaps rather quirky genius might indeed have worked on the hint provided by Knowlton's authors to produce his Kynde. But other suggestions can be offered. Schmidt refers to the scholastic distinction between *natura naturans* and *natura naturata* and identifies Langland's Kynde with the former.[8] *Natura naturans* became a common designation for God as creative first cause in thirteenth century scholastic writing according to which God is (unpantheisti-

---

[3] E. C. Knowlton 'Nature in Middle English', *JEGP*, 20 (1921), 186–207 (p. 198).
[4] *Ibid.*
[5] *Ibid.*
[6] That Langland's Kynde is (orthodoxly) distinct from his creation should be sufficiently apparent from the opening quotation of this chapter.
[7] For Stoic influence on the Middle Ages and its channels (mainly Seneca and Cicero) see G. Verbecke, 'L'Influence du Stoïcisme sur la Pensée Médiévale en Occident' in *Actas del 5. Congreso Internacional de Filosofía Medieval* (Madrid, 1979), 95–109.
[8] Schmidt (1987), on IX 2, p. 327.

cally) distinguished from the world of created beings, *natura naturata*.[9] Now, 'nature' can have reference to a particular individual item or to the order of things in general. One suspects the former in *natura naturans* because a general reference for *natura* in that phrase seems too limiting for God – God can legitimately be seen as a creative nature, but to identify him even with something as vast as the creative principle inherent in the natural world is to fail to mark God's transcendence of the natural world, to confuse creature and creator in precisely the manner the scholastic distinction seeks to avoid.[10] Clearly the designation *natura naturans*, even understood as 'the (individual) nature which creates', must, especially in conjunction with its twin phrase, bring to mind God's presidence over the natural world, general nature. However, the structure of the phrase sets a distance between this nature and what it creates, and the fact that what is created is not actually specified works to the same end. This does not seem to accord well with the direct reference to general nature in Langland's term Kynde, a reference which must exist if Kynde is not to lack all definition.[11] Langland's designation goes so far as to define God with reference to the natural world, at this semantic level involving him more closely than does the scholastic term in his creation.[12] Langland certainly could have arrived at his Kynde through collapsing *natura naturans* into one word which can easily bear the meaning 'power presiding over the created realm' (and the alliteration of Kynde with

---

[9] On the *natura naturans* / *natura naturata* terminology see H. Siebeck, 'Ueber die Enstehung der Termini natura naturans und natura naturata', *Archiv für Geschichte der Philosophie*, 3 (1890), 370–8; H. A. Lucks, 'Natura Naturans – Natura Naturata', *The New Scholasticism*, 9 (1935) 1–24; O. Weijers, 'Contribution à l'histoire des termes "natura naturans" et "natura naturata"', *Vivarium*, 16 (1978), 70–80.

[10] Tierney (1963), p. 317, relates the *natura naturans* notion to Augustine's talk of God as *a* creative nature. See also the citations from Barthelémy de Bologne, Pierre de Falco and Ramon Lull in Weijers (1978), pp. 73–4. However, frequently one would be unable to determine the sense of *natura* in a particular usage of *natura naturans* simply from a consideration of that usage and its immediate context.

[11] One wonders whether Julian of Norwich's use of *kynde* might be relevant for Langland's figure Kynde. At one point (*A Book of the Showings to the Anchoress Julian of Norwich*, ed. E. Colledge and J. Walsh (Toronto, 1978), p. 611) Julian remarks

God is kynd in his being; that is to sey the goodnesse that is kynd, it is god.

It is by no means clear how this sentence should be construed grammatically and hence by no means clear what it means, but we may well have an identification of God with *kynd*. For Julian God appears to be the ground of all existent things, all *kynd(s)* (see *Showings* pp. 611–12). A basis for Langland's figure might be found here, but the active creativity of Kynde would not seem obviously accountable for in terms of Julian's usage. In any case, Julian's formulation seems rather idiosyncratic, and on chronological grounds alone any direct influence of Julian on Langland is highly unlikely. (Colledge and Walsh (1978), p. 40, suggest that Julian might have known *Piers Plowman*.)

[12] I shall be suggesting that the semantic involvement is related to a more important involvement: problems about the *kynde* order of things very easily produce disturbing questions about a God designated Kynde. Further to this issue of the involvement of created nature and God, it

*creatour* might be thought to reflect the alliteration in the Latin), but if that is what happened the end-product is significantly different from what Langland started from.

It may be possible to propose a rather tighter process of derivation. Brian Tierney has suggested that the *natura naturans* concept had an influence on juristic discussions of the law of nature and that this influence explains how the phrase *Natura, id est Deus* came to be used by certain jurists.[13] Tierney points out that it is unlikely that this formulation would have been acceptable in so standard a text as the *Glossa Ordinaria* if it represented a stoicising pantheism.[14] He suggests that the jurists who used this phrase were thinking of Nature (and hence God) as 'a creative force that implanted in each creature its own proper mode of activity' – the *Natura, id est Deus* formulation is used to gloss the Ulpianic definition of the law of nature as *quod natura omnia animalia docuit.*[15] Such a sense of nature, Tierney claims, had been made available through scholastic use of the *natura naturans / natura naturata* terminology.[16] Tierney quotes a passage from Vincent of Beauvais[17] which uses the *natura naturans* idea, but which also defines God as the *summa lex naturae*, a definition which seems further to justify the juristic *Natura, id est Deus* because it involves God more closely in the natural realm: he is represented not simply as promulgating the law according to which the natural realm functions, but as actually being that law.

However it arises, the juristic formulation defines God as Nature (or vice versa), which the scholastic *natura naturans* seems not to do (for all that the juristic definition is explicable with reference to the scholastic terminology), and so might seem likely to have played a larger part in the production of Langland's figure.[18] Kynde in *Piers Plowman* displays certain features that

---

is interesting to find A. V. C. Schmidt contrasting the author of *The Cloud of Unknowing* to Langland and Julian of Norwich as follows:

> So totally is he [the *Cloud* author] committed to viewing *natura naturata* as radically contingent, that he cannot share Julian's and Langland's sense of nature as participating in the being of the creator, . . . .

('Langland and the Mystical Tradition' in *The Medieval Mystical Tradition in England*, ed. Marion Glasscoe (Exeter, 1980), 17–38 (p. 35)).

[13] Tierney (1963).
[14] *Ibid.*, pp. 308–9.
[15] *Ibid.*, p. 316 and for the glossing of the Ulpianic definition, p. 314.
[16] *Ibid.*, p. 317.
[17] *Ibid.*, p. 317. The passage (from the *Speculum Maius*) runs as follows:

> In summa vero nota quod natura primo dicitur dupliciter. Uno modo natura naturans, id est ipsa summa lex naturae quae Deus est. . . . Aliter vero dicitur natura naturata et haec multipliciter.

[18] Langland's 'many legal references' (Baldwin (1981), p. 2) seem to establish the possibility of his having been acquainted with the *Natura, id est Deus* formulation.

might be accounted for by supposing that Langland had a legal context in mind when creating his figure. Thus at B XII 225ff. Ymaginatif, reviewing the vision of *Myddelerthe*, speaks of Kynde as one who teaches the animals, which might be referred to the Ulpianic definition of the law of nature, as might Kynde's concern here with procreation.[19] Further, Langland might have been stimulated to the paradoxical contrast of the 'irrational' animals *sewed* by Reason and 'rational' man whom Reason does not follow by the conflicting definitions of natural law (in terms of instinct on the one hand and reason on the other) found in the body of medieval writings on that subject.[20]

Nevertheless, these features can also be explained with reference to another kind of writing, the Chartrian tradition of personification allegory. In this tradition the Nature figure is much concerned with the perpetuation of species through procreation, and procreation is part of what she teaches the animals. The tradition speaks too of the failure of man to follow his reason, which leads him into disobedience to Nature, a disobedience exhibited by man alone of all that goddess' creatures.[21] One would not wish to suggest, in any case, that the juristic tradition and the Chartrian writings were completely distinct.[22] And, of course, Langland may have developed his Kynde from suggestions provided by more than one source. The important thing is to be alive to the possibility that the figure has certain resonances because of its relations with other Natures from whatever strain of writing.

So, though Langland's Kynde must not be seen simply as a further example of the Chartrian Nature figure, it is very possible that Langland's conception owes something to this tradition. Langland may well have known the writings of Alan of Lille and the *Roman de la Rose*.[23] Langland may have

[19] See also B XI 334ff. where the Dreamer contemplates the 'engendrynge of kynde' and related activities among the animals and birds in his vision of Kynde's world.

[20] Commenting on various definitions of the law of nature drawn from the *Digest* and the *Institutes* (and also from Gratian's *Decretum*) Azo (*Summa Institutionum* I, 2, cited Carlyle (1903–36) Vol. 2, p. 30, n. 1) distinguishes the Ulpianic definition from the others as follows:

> Prima autem definitio [Ulpian's] data est secundum motum sensualitatis, aliae autem assignatae sunt secundum modum rationis.

[21] See *De Planctu Naturae* VIII 10–18 and *Roman de la Rose* 18917ff.

[22] Alan of Lille was a theologian who had occasion in his theological dictionary, the *Distinctiones*, to give a definition of the law of nature. It is obvious that the legal tradition owes much to the theologians.

[23] According to Schmidt (1987) pp. 233, 353, Langland was acquainted with Alan's *Liber Parabolarum*, and he may well also have known the apparently more popular *De Planctu Naturae* and the *Anticlaudianus*. For the possible influence of the *Roman de la Rose* on *Piers Plowman* see D. L. Owen, *Piers Plowman, A Comparison with some Earlier and Contemporary French Allegories* (London, 1912), especially pp. 53–6, 82–5, 118–19, 127–8. Pp. 84–5, 118–19 and 128 deal with possible influences of the *Roman de la Rose* on Langland's Kynde. Pp. 118–19 mention Nature's complaint in the *Roman* that Man alone of all the animals fails to follow her directions and compare the failure of Man in Langland's *Myddelerthe* passage to act reasonably. A similar complaint is made by Natura in the *De Planctu* (see note 21). Chartrian influence seems very possible here.

seen his figure as a kind of counterblast to the Chartrian goddess – the immediate differences are certainly very striking.[24] And besides creating a startlingly innovative contrast to the Chartrian Nature in making his Kynde not only masculine but also God himself, Langland may be playing off his figure against the Chartrian goddess in other less obvious ways.

The Chartrian Nature is, very broadly, a life-giving figure. Langland's Kynde is interested in the preservation of the *kynde* of his creatures and appears, like the Chartrian figure, to sponsor sexual activity with a view to procreation.[25] But, at least at a superficial level, the Chartrian Nature's strenuous opposition of death in the interests of the continuation of physical life[26] appears to bring her into conflict with Langland's Kynde as he appears in Passus B XX, where he promotes death. It can, nevertheless, be suggested that the Kynde whom the C text describes as Love and everlasting Life (C X 168–9) is concerned to give life at a more important level than the merely physical. Certain piquant overtones are created by the contrast with the Chartrian figure who battles against physical death.

In Alan of Lille's *De Planctu Naturae* Nature laments that man is the only one of her creatures who fails to obey her and it is made clear that this failure is due to man's rejection of reason.[27] Not to follow reason is not to follow Nature. The relation between Nature and Reason later in the tradition which derives from the twelfth-century Chartrian writings is not always so harmonious. Nature's sponsorship of the instinctual side of man draws her away, in some writers' treatments, from Reason.[28] This kind of treatment of Nature may have influenced Chaucer in the *Parlement of Foules*, though his distinction between reason and nature in that poem is not simply a counterposing of the rational and the instinctual. The refusal of the formel eagle to choose between the three tercels appears to image a natural irrationality in man. Nature permits the exercise of free will, and this can mean a falling away from the course of action Reason would dictate. Nature rather hesitantly advises the formel to take the royal tercel, prefacing this

---

[24] An acquaintance with the Chartrian goddess, who appears in a number of well-diffused medieval texts, would not have been particularly recondite: Langland could reasonably have expected at least some of his audience to register the ways in which his Kynde differed from the Chartrian Nature.

[25] The *Myddelerthe* vision is much concerned with procreation: see B XI 334ff. There appears also to be testimony to the concern of Kynde with the preservation of life (physical rather than spiritual) when Wit informs us that

lyf lyueth by inwit and leryng of Kynde; . . . .

(C X 172)

[26] Though Nature is responsible for death at *Roman de la Rose* 16945ff., for instance, the main weight of the Chartrian tradition insists on her determination that procreation shall occur.

[27] *De Planctu Naturae* II 234ff. and VI 51ff.

[28] Thus in the *Roman de la Rose* Nature countenances Venus-sponsored love of which Reason disapproves. See also, for instance, *Renart le Contrefait*, ed. G. Raynaud and H. Lemaître (Paris, 1914), 24367ff.

advice with 'If I were Resoun',[29] a hint which seems to require us to be well aware of the fact that she is not Reason and that she countenances the irrational. Man's natural capacity of free choice is something he has in virtue of his rationality, but it certainly will not always lead him to follow Reason in the sense of the reasonable and right. Somewhat similarly, Langland presents a picture of the realm of Kynde in which the unreasonable behaviour of man is permitted by the presiding deity, not complained about as it is by the Nature of the *De Planctu*. The complaining, interestingly enough, is done by Will who rebukes Reason for his failure to follow man:

> I have wonder of thee, that witty art holden,
> Why thow ne sewest man and his make, that no mysfeet hem folwe.

(B XI 373–4)

Again, this situation carries considerable ironic resonance if aligned with the *De Planctu* in which it is man who fails to follow reason rather than Reason who fails to follow man.

These suggestions about the derivation of Langland's figure should not lead us to overlook the fact that his Kynde is indeed something rather strange and apparently new in medieval poetry. Why, we might ask, should Langland feel impelled to identify Nature and God? The Chartrian picture of Nature in subordination to God is well equipped to accommodate a sense of the imperfection of the natural order, as is perhaps to be expected in view of the neoplatonic, emanationist origins of the Chartrian literary myths.[30] The unsatisfactoriness of things in the realm of Nature does not redound directly upon God. God is ultimately responsible for the arrangements Nature makes, but in the space between God and Nature, as it were, we can imagine God working through other means in an activity which can be set against the activity he conducts through Nature and through which he may compensate for the defects apparent in Nature's work. The perceived defects of the natural order can, in fact, be settled comfortably on a Nature with whom it is understood the whole story does not end. But if, conversely, one wished to affirm strongly the essential rightness of the way things naturally are, one might close the gap between God and the created world, as Langland does. To do this, though, has repercussions. When there is no available space between God and Nature in which God can be imagined working out his benign purposes in possibly rather mysterious ways, the question of justifying the evil apparent in the natural realm is much more pressing. The problem of natural evil cannot be shelved on the strength of a

---

[29] *The Parlement of Foules* 632.
[30] On these origins see T. Gregory, *Anima Mundi, La filosofia di Guglielmo di Conches e la scuola di Chartres* (Firenze, 1955); T. Gregory, *Platonismo Medievale* (Roma, 1958); B. Stock, *Myth and Science in the Twelfth Century, A Study of Bernard Silvester* (Princeton, 1972); W. Wetherbee, *Platonism and Poetry in the Twelfth Century* (Princeton, 1972).

sense that God stands above Nature and may be tacitly understood to be working behind her, correcting what she is doing, and we cannot shuffle the blame off onto an inferior power. God is in no way distanced from the unsatisfactoriness of the natural realm, may even be thought of as endorsing this, and we are strongly impelled to demand what he is doing in acting thus. This is, of course, a question Will eventually asks (though indirectly) of Kynde.[31] The different implications in Chartrian 'separatist' treatments and Langland's appear clearly if we consider the relations between the Nature figure and the reasonable. As has been mentioned above, certain later writings in which a recognisably Chartrian Nature appears present a conflict between Nature and Reason. This is not necessarily all that disturbing since such an arrangement suggests that the evil laid up in Nature can be opposed if man follows Reason, and that this should be required of man can be understood to be an ultimately beneficent arrangement of God, who may be thought of as manipulating, for his own good ends a Nature to whom he stands superior.[32] But where, as in Langland, the Nature which (at least when man is considered) permits and perhaps encourages unreasonable behaviour – Kynde could easily, after all, have arranged for Reason to *sewe* man – is identified with God, the problem of evil immediately appears much more difficult.

This is to suggest that a desire to see the natural as good prompted Langland's identification of God and Nature, but that certain difficulties are latent in this manoeuvre. The suggestion gains some support from the fact that in Langland's first extended consideration of Kynde the Creator an assertion of the satisfactoriness of the basic ontological condition of mankind is indeed being made. The passage occurs already in the A version. It is only with the *Myddelerthe* vision, new to the B version of the poem, that the order established by Kynde is explicitly questioned. Perhaps certain difficulties not bargained for when the identification of Kynde and God was made had by the time of the B version become apparent to Langland and seemed to require attention. Further, the C revisions of Wit's discourse on Kynde may reflect an increasing dissatisfaction on Langland's part with his initial treatment of Kynde.[33]

But for whatever reason the identification is made, it seems eventually to

[31] See B XI 368–74. Phillipa Tristram, *Figures of Life and Death in Medieval English Literature* (London, 1976), p. 53, thinks that in schemes with a separate Nature questions as to the beneficence of the natural order become more difficult, the reverse of my contention.

[32] Somewhat similarly Nature in the *De Planctu Naturae* has arranged within man a conflict between *ratio* and *sensualitas*, requiring man to free himself from the dominance of the latter and to pursue the former (see VI 51–4, 66–8 and also II 232–4). The benevolence of this kind of arrangement depends on it really being possible for man to free himself from the influence of the dubious antagonist: one wonders to what extent Gower, who in *Confessio Amantis* presents a conflict between the demands reason and *kinde* make upon man, believes men can free themselves from the influence of *kinde*.

[33] See below.

demand a theodicy dealing with the operations of God as instigator and superintendent of the realm of the natural. A theodical concern is, I think, present in the second and third Kynde episodes, as Langland struggles to see the apparently disastrous aspects of man's natural condition as good, as conducive to salvation. But it is time now to examine the three major Kynde sequences in more detail.

It is Wit who first introduces Kynde. He does so in his explanation of where Dowel dwells, an explanation that involves a sketch of the basic condition of mankind. This is something for which Kynde is responsible:

> 'Sire Dowel dwelleth,' quod Wit, 'noght a day hennes
> In a castel that Kynde made of foure kynnes thynges.
> Of erthe and eyr is it maad, medled togideres,
> With wynd and with water wittily enjoyned.
> Kynde hath closed therinne craftily withalle
> A lemman that he loveth lik to hymselve
> *Anima* she hatte; . . . .'

(B IX 1–7)

The devil seeks to win her away, but *Anima* is protected from his assaults by Dowel, Dobet and Dobest and Inwit and his five sons until such time as

> Kynde come or sende to kepen hire hymselve.

(B IX 24)

When the dreamer asks 'What kynnes thyng is Kynde?' (B IX 25), Wit makes the identification of Kynde with God the Creator explicit:

> 'Kynde,' quod Wit, 'is creatour of alle kynnes thynges,
> Fader and formour of al that evere was maked –
> And that is the grete God that gynnyng hadde nevere,
> Lord of lif and of light, of lisse and of peyne.
> Aungeles and alle thyng arn at his wille,
> Ac man is hym moost lik of marc and of shape. . . .'

(B IX 26–31)

The statement that man is of all creatures most like God confirms the optimistic perspective on man as he is by Kynde presented up to this point in all three versions. At this point, however, C qualifies this optimism by saying that sin destroys the soul's likeness to God.[34] In A and B there is no suggestion that *Anima* may fail in her likeness to God. Evil is concentrated in the figure of the *Princeps huius mundi*, and *Anima*'s guardians seem sufficient to repel his attacks. For her part, *Anima* appears to accept the ruling of Dobest and Inwit without demur. Man's natural condition, according to Wit in A and B, is to be set amidst evils but successfully to resist their pressure, and we might interpret Dowel's presence within the Kynde-established *Caro* as indicating that virtue is natural to man. Later in his

---

[34] C X 157 reads 'And semblable in soule to god but if synne hit make.' Tristram (1976), p. 53, is still able to accuse C's Wit of (over-) simplification.

discourse, Wit concedes that *inwit* can be misruled, but he seems to think, at least in A and B, that if this is avoided temptations to sin can be smoothly negotiated.

The optimistic view of man as he is by Kynde is evident also in the following – C has no equivalent – which treats further Kynde's creation of man:

> And thus God gaf hym a goost, of the godhede of hevene,
> And of his grete grace graunted hym blisse –
> And that is lif that ay shal laste to al his lynage after.
> And that is the castel that Kynde made, *Caro* it hatte,
> And is as muche to mene as "man with a soule."
>
> (B IX 46–50)

In Kynde's disposition of things man is destined for bliss. There may also be a suggestion that God's grace is, as it were, natural to man, seeing that God as Kynde is disposed to grant bliss of his grace. Grace could, in the perspective that Wit offers, be seen as an item in nature. Optimism of this sort is appropriate in a consideration of man prior to the Fall, and the passage just quoted is taken from a context which deals with God's first creation, but Wit appears to intend his allegory of the Castle of *Caro* and *Anima* to have relevance to the post-Fall world; after all, he says that the Castle of *Caro* is not a day's journey away. We may suppose that Wit is presenting a picture of how things should *ideally* operate in Kynde's realm, but one is still inclined to ask whether Wit understands the consequences of the Fall. Wit seems to suggest that *blisse* has been granted to all the descendants of Adam, which is to ignore the damnation presumably in prospect for some as a result of the Fall.[35] Further, we may wonder how adequate a view of man's condition it is to suppose that, providing the intellectual capacities function properly,[36] the soul remains safe from the assaults of sin, having the ability to insulate itself, as it were, from the effects of the Fall.

Wit makes much use of *kynde* terms, as if man's condition and the business of salvation can be adequately analysed with reference to the *kynde*. Wit speaks of God as Kynde and he employs *kynde* related notions extensively in his discussion of evil: one must not misrule the Kynde-given *inwit* through drink, no Christian creature should be *unkynde* to another, and all evil deeds seem to result from *unkynde* marriages which, like those contracted between Caym's *kynde* and Seem's, are against God's will, or from a failure to observe the proper times for sexual activity.[37] Though Wit

---

[35] Later in the poem Langland comes at least very close to announcing through his figure of Christ in Passus B XVIII a doctrine of universal salvation (see chapter 4, note 34), but that position is articulated only after considerable debate over the issue, and I doubt we should accept the unorthodoxy from Wit's mouth here.

[36] On *inwit* see Quirk (1953). At B XV 16ff. *Anima*, describing himself, does not separate the soul and the intellectual faculties, which are an aspect (or aspects) of the soul.

[37] B IX 60–6a, B IX 84, B IX 119ff. particularly 153–7, B IX 184ff.

remarks that 'after the grace of God, the gretteste is Inwit' (B IX 59) it may
be asked whether he gives sufficient weight to grace and man's need for it
(we remember the B IX 46–50 passage with its possible assimilation of grace
to the realm of the natural). But the blame may lie with Langland rather
than with Wit: a concern on the poet's part to affirm the rightness of the
natural may lead to oversimplification, to naive optimism. Certainly, C's
changes strongly suggest that Langland found the optimism of the initial
treatment of Kynde unsatisfactory. We might here recall the fate *kynde wit*
suffers as the poem develops.

Kynde next appears (in Passus B XI) as a character in the dream action of
the poem. Earlier in the Passus Will has been seduced by Fortune, and
Trajan has appeared and delivered a long and somewhat disorderly diatribe:

> and sithen cam Kynde
> And nempned me by my name, and bad me nymen hede,
> And thorugh the wondres of this world wit for to take.
> And on a mountaigne that Myddelerthe highte, as me tho thoughte,
> I was fet forth by ensaumples to knowe,
> Thorugh ech a creature, Kynde my creatour to lovye.
>
> (B XI 320–5)

It has been suggested that Kynde here stands parallel to Fortune.[38] This
parallelism might reflect a traditional medieval distinction between Nature
and Fortune according to which what Fortune gives is seen as inauthentic in
comparison with Nature's provisions.[39] Fortune had fetched Will into the
'lond of longynge and love' and got him to look in the 'mirour that highte
Middelerthe' to see *wondres* (B XI 8–10). In Fortune's presentation, the
wonders of the world were objects for Will's concupiscence, stimulating
attachment to the material, but when they are presented by their Creator,
who may be expected to set them in the proper light, they are, it is
suggested, objects for the Dreamer's knowledge, *ensaumples* displaying
God's ways and stimulating love of him.

Kynde is the Creator, and what Will sees is a panorama of creation. He
finds in it a wonderful, indeed miraculous, copiousness and variety:

> And sithen I loked on the see and so forth on the sterres;
> Manye selkouthes I seigh, ben noght to seye nouthe.
> I seigh floures in the fryth and hir faire colours,
> And how among the grene gras growed so manye hewes,
> And some soure and some swete – selkouth me thoghte.
>
> (B XI 362–6)

---

[38] J. S. Wittig, ' "Piers Plowman" B, Passus IX–XII: Elements in the Design of the Inward
*Journey'*, *Traditio*, 28 (1972), 211–80.
[39] See B. Bartholomew, *Fortuna and Natura: A Reading of Three Chaucer Narratives* (The
Hague, 1966), pp. 12–24.

He has seen too an admirable reasonableness and purposiveness in the behaviour of the animals, so that he is led to wonder who is finally responsible:

> Reson I seigh soothly sewen alle beestes
> In etynge, in drynkynge and in engendrynge of kynde.
> And after cours of concepcion noon took kepe of oother
> As whan thei hadde ryde in rotey tyme; anoonright therafter
> Males drowen hem to males amornynge by hemselve,
> And [femelles to femelles ferded and drowe].
> Ther ne was cow ne cowkynde that conceyved hadde
> That wolde belwe after bole, ne boor after sowe.
> Bothe hors and houndes and alle othere beestes
> Medled noght with hir makes that [mid] fole were.
>   Briddes I biheld that in buskes made nestes;
> Hadde nevere wye wit to werche the leeste.
> I hadde wonder at whom and wher the pye
> Lerned to legge the stikkes in which she leyeth and bredeth.
> Ther nys wrighte, as I wene, sholde werche hir nest to paye;
> If any mason made a molde therto, muche wonder it were.
>   And yet me mervveilled moore: many othere briddes
> Hidden and hileden hir egges ful derne
> In mareys and moores for men sholde hem noght fynde,
> And hidden hir egges whan thei therfro wente,
> For fere of othere foweles and for wilde beestes.
>   And some troden hir makes and on trees bredden
> And broughten forth hir briddes so al above the grounde.
> And some briddes at the bile thorugh brethyng conceyved,
> And some caukede; I took kepe how pecokkes bredden.
> Muche mervveilled me what maister thei hadde,
> And who taughte hem on trees to tymbre so heighe
> That neither burn ne beest may hir briddes rechen.

(B XI 334–61)

The answer to the question who has taught the beasts their behaviour is evident to the reader from what Will says about the purpose of his vision, but it may be that we should consider the experiencing Dreamer (as opposed to the reporting poet) answered only in the following Passus when Ymaginatif tells him that Kynde is responsible for the arrangements of the natural world.[40] The gap between vision and explanation draws attention to the fact that the explanation is one that does not arise automatically, and this may suggest that there is something problematic in what Will sees (I address this issue below). In any case, when Will reflects at the beginning of Passus B XIII on his recent experiences, his knowledge of Kynde is said to have been delivered by Ymaginatif. And Ymaginatif's comments on Kynde, here

---

[40] B XII 217–35. Richard of St Victor says that the *imaginatio* wonders at the things of the visible world and at the munificent creativity of God revealed in them (*Benjamin Major* I ch. 6; PL 196, 70).

summarised and drawn out, are presented as an unfolding of Will's vision of
the world of Kynde. Will recalls

> how that Ymaginatif in dremels me tolde
> Of Kynde and of his konnynge, and how curteis he is to bestes,
> And how lovynge he is to bestes on londe and on watre:
> Leneth he no lif lasse ne moore;
> The creatures that crepen of Kynde ben engendred;
>
> (B XIII 14–18)

The contemplation of the world of nature reveals God's *konnynge* and his
*curteisie*. One might relate the copiousness and variety of creation and the
reasonableness and purposiveness of the animals to God's *konnynge*. One
can discern a sort of argument from design displaying God in his power and
reason. There is in this of itself reason to love God. But there is further
cause for this love in God's *curteisie* and love towards all creatures. This
*curteisie* and love seem in the B text to be expressed in the provision of the
means of physical livelihood for all creatures. The link between God's love
and what he provides is more explicit in C:

> . . . . Kynde and his connynge, and what connynge he ʒaf bestes,
> And how louyng he is to vch a lyf, a londe and o watere,
> For alle a wisseth and ʒeueth wit þat walketh oþer crepeth.
>
> (C XV 18–20)

An earlier passage in C suggests that the provision of wit is related to
physical survival. It is Kynde who teaches

> Adam and Eue and alle othere bestes
> A cantel of kynde wyt here kynde to saue.
>
> (C XIV 162–3)[41]

This is part of the contrivance of Kynde in his disposition of the world of
nature, a contrivance said to have been effected 'of his corteyse wille'
(C XIV 160).

There may be another aspect to Kynde's *curteisie*. In contrast to Wit's
picture of what man is by Kynde, Passus B XI offers an unidealistic view of
man under Kynde, drawing attention to man's unreasonableness by setting it
against the behaviour of the brute creation which is *sewed* by Reason. Yet

---

[41] It is possible that 'here kynde to saue' should be taken as having reference to the preserva-
tion of the species through procreation, especially in view of the line preceding the quoted
passage:

> He tauhte þe tortle to trede, the pocok to cauke, . . . .
>
> (C XIV 161)

But earlier in the C text (X 172ff.) Wit affirms, in terms rather similar to those of the present
passage, that *lyf* (in contradistinction to *Anima*) lives 'by inwit and leryng of Kynde' where what
appears to be at stake is the preservation of an individual rather than the species. *Kynde* can
mean 'vital forces' and may well bear that meaning at C XIV 163, the preservation of the
individual through the use of certain equipment possessed naturally then being in view.

man is part of Kynde's realm, and his unreasonableness is permitted by Kynde for larger purposes. Reason, attacked by Will for failing to *sewe* man, says this:

> 'Who suffreth moore than God?' . . . . 'no gome, as I leeve.
> He myghte amende in a minute while al that mysstandeth,
> Ac he suffreth for som mannes goode, and so is oure bettre. . . .'
>
> (B XI 379–81)

It would seem that contemplation of the world of Kynde and therefore of man in a certain perspective can lead to an awareness of the charitable long-suffering of God, an awareness that might be expected to lead to love of God.

Contemplation of the natural world with its pointers to the qualities of God is not, however, guaranteed to lead to such a love, and here we arrive at the problematic quality of the vision at which I hinted earlier. The purpose of the vision on *Myddelerthe* was, we have been told (B XI 323–5),[42] to lead Will to love of his Creator, but the Dreamer's perception of evil in the world of Kynde instead drives him to object to the disposition of that world:

> Ac that moost meved me and my mood chaunged –
> That Reson rewarded and ruled alle beestes
> Save man and his make: many tyme and ofte
> No Reson hem folwede, [neither riche ne povere].
> And thanne I rebukede Reson, and right til hymselven I seyde,
>   'I have wonder of thee, that witty art holden,
> Why thow ne sewest man and his make, that no mysfeet hem folwe.'
>
> (B XI 368–74)

Raising as it does the problem of evil, the *Myddelerthe* vision is in danger of proving utterly *un*conducive to love of God. Reason, of course, asserts that evil exists because of God's *curteisie* towards man, but he is not capable of more than assertion. He says

> For be a man fair or foul, it falleth noght to lakke
> The shap ne the shaft that God shoop hymselve;
> For al that he wrought was wel ydo, as Holy Writ witnesseth:
> *Et vidit Deus cuncta que fecerat, et erant valde bona.*
>
> (B XI 394–6a)

For all this, what immediately follows seems to accord ultimate responsibility for the evil in man to God who made him and gave him his *kynde*:

> And bad every creature in his kynde encreesse,
> Al to murthe with man that moste wo tholie
> In fondynge of the flessh and of the fend bothe.
> For man was maad of swich a matere he may noght wel asterte
> That som tyme hym bitit to folwen his kynde.
> Caton acordeth therwith – *Nemo sine crimine vivit!*
>
> (B XI 397–402)

---

[42] In C (XIII 130–2) Kynde makes Rechelesnesse look in the mirror of *Mydelerthe*.

In the quotation with which he prefaces these remarks Reason would appear to acknowledge that God's purposes in creating some things *foul* and in building in evil tendencies to man's nature are unfathomable:

*De re que te non molestat noli certare.*[43]

(B XI 393)

Reason's remarks present a strong contrast to the easy clarity of Wit's discourse on Kynde.

In Passus B XII Ymaginatif is very emphatic about the unfathomability of God's activity. He concentrates on the ultimate inexplicability of phenomena in the realm of natural science rather than on the theological issue of the problem of evil, but he connects his discourse with Will's rebuke of Reason, which was a response to the perception of evil in Kynde's world, so that his remarks on the hiddenness of the *whyes* in the realm of natural science may be felt to have a wider reference to God's fundamental disposition of things in general:

> And so I seye by thee, that sekest after the whyes,
> And aresonedest Reson, a rebukynge as it were,
> And willest of briddes and of beestes and of hir bredyng knowe,
> Why some be alough and some aloft, thi likyng it were;
> And of the floures in the fryth and of hire faire hewes –
> Wherof thei cacche hir colours so clere and so brighte,
> And of the stones and of the sterres – thow studiest, as I leve,
> How evere beest outher brid hath so breme wittes. . . .
>     Clergie ne Kynde Wit ne knew nevere the cause,
> Ac Kynde knoweth the cause hymself and no creature ellis.
> He is the pies patron and putteth it in hir ere
> That there the thorn is thikkest to buylden and brede.
> And Kynde kenned the pecok to cauken in swich a kynde,
> And Kynde kenned Adam to knowe his pryve membres,
> And taughte hym and Eve to helien hem with leves.
>     Lewed men many tymes maistres thei apposen,
> Whi Adam ne hiled noght first his mouth that eet the appul,
> Rather than his likame alogh? – lewed asken thus clerkes.
> Kynde knoweth whi he dide so, ac no clerk ellis!

(B XII 217–35)

In the equivalent passage in the C text, the issue of evil is more clearly involved in the unfathomability of God's *whyes* than it is in B. This passage is also explicit on the permission Kynde gives to evil, and the line 'Of goed and of wykke Kynde was þe furste' seems unequivocally to indicate his ultimate responsibility for it:

---

[43] The point here is not, I think, that God is not responsible for the evil in the world which is committed by man, as Wittig (1972), p. 243, suggests. God is, after all, explicitly given responsibility for the *foul*ness of which B XI 394–6a speaks. Reason implicitly acknowledges the difficulty of explaining evil which any argument from design must encounter, but asserts that nevertheless God's creation is good.

> And so y sey by þe þat sekest aftur þe whyes
> How creatures han kynde wit and how clerkes come to bokes
> And how þe floures in þe fryth cometh to fayre hewes;
> Was neuere creature vnder Crist þat knewe wel þe bygynnyng
> Bote Kynde þat contreuede hit furst of his corteyse wille.
> He tauhte þe tortle to trede, the pocok to cauke,
> And Adam and Eue and alle othere bestes
> A cantel of kynde wyt here kynde to saue.
> Of goed and of wykke Kynde was þe furste,
> Sey hit and soffred hit and saide hit be sholde.
> > *Dixit et facta sunt.*
> Ac why a wolde þat wykke were, y wene and y leue
> Was neuere man vppon molde þat myhte hit aspie.

> (C XIV 156–67)

For Ymaginatif, the impossibility of answering these questions implies that man should not be concerned with them, as Reason had asserted.

Later, *Anima* will rebuke Will for his desire to know everything (B XV 50ff.), and in his attitude to the world of Kynde Will seems open to the charge of gratuitous intellectual curiosity: if under Fortune the wonders of the world were objects for Will's cupidity, under Kynde they can still, apparently, be misappropriated, this time by an acquisitive intellect desirous of knowledge for its own sake.[44] The continuation of the passages just quoted points to a proper way of using observations of the world of Kynde:

> Ac of briddes and of beestes men by olde tyme
> Ensamples token and termes, as telleth thise poetes,
> And that the faireste fowel foulest engendreth,
> And feblest fowel of flight is that fleeth or swymmeth.
> And that is the pecok and the pehen – proude riche men thei bitokneth.

> (B XII 236–40)

As we saw in Chapter 1, natural phenomena may have a symbolic value that can be mobilised for the moral education of men. This symbolic value might be taken as another aspect of the provision for his creatures made by God evident in the natural world, a provision which demonstrates God's *curteisie* and love.[45]

But though Will's zoological interests can perhaps be dismissed as so

---

[44] But see Mann (1979), pp. 41f.

[45] At C XVIII 215–39 Faith uses 'The werkes þat hymsulue [God] wrouhte and this world bothe' (214) to explain God's nature as a Trinity in Unity. He speaks of the *kynde* order in respect of reproduction and love:

> And man withoute a make myhte nat wel of kynde
> Multiplie ne moreouer withoute a make louye
> Ne withoute a soware be suche seed, this we seen alle.

> (C XVIII 224–6)

This kind of symbolic use of the natural is common in medieval texts. Examples may be found in *Medieval English Sermons*, ed. W. O. Ross, *EETS* o.s. 209 (London, 1940), p. 262, lines 30ff. and p. 264, lines 34ff.

much empty *curiositas*, his worry about the evil apparent in Kynde's realm raises legitimate and disturbing questions. One such question concerns the efficacy of the kind of contemplation with which Will has been provided. With the vision of *Myddelerthe* as interpreted by Ymaginatif Langland suggests that a contemplation of the natural world can lead to an awareness of the power and majesty, the wisdom and love of God. This may be expected to lead to love of God by man. But Ymaginatif's explanation arrives *after* the contemplation, and the Dreamer's rebuking of Reason makes clear that that contemplation leaves room for doubt about the goodness of what God has done in creation. One may, in fact, be left questioning God's disposition, not fully acknowledging the absoluteness of God's love, and so remaining unloving oneself.

This whole episode is perhaps to be seen in close relation to the debate about the worth of learning which is prominent in the early Passus of the B continuation. Ymaginatif, for all his support of Clergie and Kynde Wit, is aware of the limitations of both of them. The vision of *Myddelerthe* may be taken as providing *kynde wit*, which B XII 67 informs us is derived from *quod vidimus*, and *kynde wit*, according to Ymaginatif, is inadequate to bring a man to Christendom and so to salvation (B XII 105–8). It is not clear that the *Myddelerthe* vision can of itself lead to a full love of God emerging from a correct appreciation of his nature and in particular His love for us, since through this *kynde wit* Will has discovered a worrying lack of reasonableness in man's behaviour under Kynde. It is worth noting that even after Ymaginatif's explanations Will wakes 'witlees nerhande', and when he introduces his next dream, he speaks of it as sent to *conforte* him, as if the years of reflection on the dream experiences of Passus B XI and XII have not led to any spiritually satisfactory conclusions:

> And I awaked therwith, witlees nerhande,
> And as a freke that fey were, forth gan I walke
> In manere of a mendynaunt many yer after,
> And of this metyng many tyme muche thought I hadde: . . . .
> I lay down longe in this thoght, and at the laste I slepte;
> And as Crist wolde ther com Conscience to conforte me that tyme. . . .
> (B XIII 1–4, 21–2)

When comfort eventually arrives, it involves a movement from Clergie to Patience, from knowledge to practice: Conscience leaves Clergie to go on pilgrimage with Patience. This perhaps validates in some degree Will's response to the *Myddelerthe* vision. His difficulties with it may reflect an awareness on Langland's part that the status of learning in respect of the pursuit of salvation is problematic.[46] In the light of this, it seems significant

---

[46] At B XI 140 Trajan begins his intervention with 'Ye, baw for bokes!', and Conscience is dismissive of Clergie's books at B XIII 200–1; yet even at that point Conscience acknowledges the truth of Clergie's prediction that the time will come when Conscience desires Clergie's counsel. That time arrives at B XX 228–9.

that Will's next encounter with Kynde has him not merely witnessing but suffering Kynde's activities.

Langland's association of his Nature figure with the unreasonable and the sinful would not have commended itself to the earlier Chartrian writers, who see man's sinfulness as a departure from both Reason and Nature. And whilst Jean de Hautville's Architrenius can reprove Nature for creating him without defence against sin, the Nature of Jean's poem indicates that this is a false complaint: she has scattered her benefits on man; his sinfulness is his own, and no responsibility for it is to be ascribed to her.[47] In Langland, on the other hand, it is part of the natural dispensation that Reason should not *sewe* man, and Kynde is seen to be responsible for *wykke* as well as *goed*. Will's complaint meets only the faithful assertions of those who can see but a limited way into God's purposes, though these have some objective backing in the provision of the means of physical livelihood evident in the natural world and suggestive of a God who cares for his creatures. Langland's picture here also stands in strong contrast with Wit's scheme in Passus B IX in which man's soul is provided by Kynde with adequate defences against the assaults of sin. The *Myddelerthe* sequence presents a more complex and worried view of the provision of Kynde than the earlier passage, a view with which, because it confronts so sharply what is problematic in Kynde's dispensation without offering any solution to the difficulty, it may be impossible, for all the poem's protestations on the theme of *non plus sapere quam oportet*, to rest.[48]

There is, for whatever reason, further development of the figure of Kynde in the poem. Seen against the background of the literary tradition of the goddess Nature, this development is rather surprising. Though there is from time to time a recognition that death is a process of nature and even on occasion an attributing to a personified Nature responsibility for death,[49] the tradition tends to view Nature as creative, concerned with coming to be. In *Piers Plowman* Kynde's creativity and concern for the continuation of life are clearly apparent, but the destructive elements of the scheme of secondary causation are also accommodated, and indeed highlighted, in the figure. Thus, when Kynde appears at the invocation of Conscience in Passus B XX, he is rampantly destructive, and the love for his creatures revealed by the vision on *Myddelerthe* as interpreted by Ymaginatif is by no means clearly apparent:

> Kynde Conscience tho herde, and cam out of the planetes,
> And sente forth his forreyours – feveres and fluxes,
> Coughes and cardiacles, crampes and toothaches,
> Rewmes and radegundes and roynouse scalles,

---

[47] *Architrenius*, I 216ff.; IX 213ff.
[48] See B XV 69 and also, for example, B X 450ff.
[49] See note 26. Gower also makes a personified *kinde* responsible for death; see *Confessio Amantis* III 2477.

Biles and bocches and brennynge agues,
Frenesies and foule yveles – forageres of Kynde
Hadde ypriked and prayed polles of peple;
Largeliche a legion lees hir lif soone.
  There was 'Harrow!' and 'Help! Here cometh Kynde,
With Deeth that is dredful, to undo us alle!'
  The lord that lyved after lust tho aloud cryde
After Confort, a knyght, to come and bere his baner.
'Alarme! Alarme!' quod that lord, 'ech lif kepe his owene!'
  Thanne mette thise men, er mynstrals myghte pipe,
And er heraudes of armes hadden discryved lordes,
Elde the hoore; he was in the vauntwarde,
And bar the baner bifore Deeth – bi right he it cleymede.
  Kynde cam after hym, with many kene soores,
As pokkes and pestilences – and muche peple shente;
So Kynde thorugh corrupcions kilde ful manye.
  Deeth cam dryvynge after and al to duste passhed
Kynges and knyghtes, kaysers and popes.
Lered ne lewed, he lefte no man stonde
That he hitte evene, that evere stired after.
Manye a lovely lady and [hir] lemmans knyghtes
Swowned and swelted for sorwe of Dethes dyntes.

(B XX 80–105)

Conscience calls off Kynde as Piers had earlier called off Hunger (B VI 199–
200) so that it may be seen whether the people will mend their ways. But

Fortune gan flatere thanne tho fewe that were alyve,

(B XX 110)

with the result that

Thus releyde Lif for a litel fortune,
And priked forth with Pride – preiseth he no vertue,
Ne careth noght how Kynde slow, and shal come at the laste
And kille alle erthely creature save Conscience oone.

(B XX 148–51)

As in B XI, Fortune appears in contrast with Kynde as a seductress into
frivolity away from the path of truth and virtue to which the world of Kynde
and its processes (here experienced rather than simply witnessed) point
man. This beneficent influence of the Kynde of B XX will shortly receive
clearer acknowledgement; at this stage we should register how the affirma-
tion that Conscience, man's moral power, will be preserved by Kynde points
to the love at the centre of Kynde's destructiveness: man will always retain
his capacity for moral choice and so his ability to achieve salvation.

  In the face of the relapse occasioned by Kynde's cessation of hostilities
Conscience calls in Elde:

For care Conscience tho cryde upon Elde,
And bad hym fonde to fighte and afere Wanhope.
  And Elde hente good hope, and hastiliche he shifte hym,
And wayved awey Wanhope and with Lif he fighteth.

(B XX 165–8)

79

There is the flavour of paradox about this: physical vitality and spiritual vitality appear as inimical to one another, and the approach of death seems efficacious for our spiritual life. Here perhaps is the most effective way in which the *kynde* impels us to virtue. It is under the pressure of his own natural decay that Will finds his way into Unity. He has been battered by Elde and appeals to Kynde:

> And as I seet in this sorwe, I saugh how Kynde passede,
> And deeth drogh neigh me – for drede gan I quake,
> And cryde to Kynde, 'Out of care me brynge!
> Lo! how Elde the hoore hath me biseye:
> Awreke me if youre wille be, for I wolde ben hennes!'
>
> (B XX 199–203)

In his reply Kynde commands Will to learn to love, thus making evident his concern for the moral welfare of mankind:

> 'If thow wolt be wroken, wend into Unitee,
> And hold thee there evere, til I sende for thee;
> And loke thow konne som craft er thow come thennes.'
>   'Counseille me, Kynde,' quod I, 'what craft be best to lerne?'
>   'Lerne to love,' quod Kynde, 'and leef alle othere.'
>   'How shal I come to catel so, to clothe me and to feede?'
>   'And thow love lelly, lakke shal thee nevere
> Weede ne worldly mete, while thi lif lasteth.'
>
> (B XX 204–11)

The demand that Will should enter Unity and abandon all crafts except love may remind us of what Ymaginatif says at the beginning of Passus B XII. He there tells Will that he is wasting his time on *makynges* (on a craft?) when he should be saying his Psalter and praying for those who give him bread (16–17) before it is too late. In Will's response we find a foreshadowing of his later arrival in Unity. He remarks that if someone would tell him what Dowel is

> Wolde I nevere do werk, but wende to holi chirche. . . .
>
> (B XII 27)

The condition Will stipulates is perhaps fulfilled in Kynde's recommendation of love. There is also mention at this point in B XII of pestilence and affliction such as we find depicted in Passus B XX:

> Amende thee while thow myght; thow hast ben warned ofte
> With poustees of pestilences, with poverte and with angres –
>
> (B XII 10–11)

The lines that follow connect the afflictions God visits on men with his love for them:

> And with thise bittre baleises God beteth his deere children:
> *Quem diligo, castigo.*

And David in the Sauter seith, of swiche that loveth Jesus,
*"Virga tua et baculus tuus, ipsa me consolata sunt:*
Although thow strike me with thi staf, with stikke or with yerde,
It is but murthe as for me to amende my soule."

(B XII 12–15)

In view of the parallels adduced between the opening of B XII and what happens to Will in B XX, one might have recourse to this last passage in understanding the assault on Will made by Kynde's agent Elde, and so discover in that assault testimony to Kynde's love of Will and mankind in general. In any case, Will's exposure to Kynde in B XI might be seen as the grounds of an unsuccessful attempt to produce the kind of spiritual progress in Will that the Kynde sequence in B XX, which employs similar terms, actually achieves. It has been suggested above that the inefficacy of the B XI vision is connected with its intellectual quality. It would be appropriate that the address of the B XI vision to Will's understanding should not be able to move him from his intellectualism to better living, and that this should eventually come about through experience, and not mere perception, of Kynde and his processes.[50]

Will asks Kynde to *awreke* him, and one wonders in what precisely that vengeance might consist. It may lie in a repudiation of the forces of decay and death (and therefore of sin), to which Will is obliged to submit, in the resurrection of the faithful soul to the bliss of heaven. For Langland, as for the writers in the Chartrian tradition, Kynde is perhaps fundamentally a life-giving figure, though it is not the life of this world that he is most deeply concerned to give. Conscience also asks Kynde for vengeance:

Now Kynde me avenge,
And sende me hap and heele, til I have Piers the Plowman!

(B XX 385–6)

Conscience seems to be requesting vengeance for the destruction of Unity by the forces of evil, a rather broader appeal than Will's, but God's triumph over evil will be consummated at the end of time in the general resurrection and judgement, so that the resurrection to life is an element that would bring together the vengeances of Will and Conscience.

We have seen that Langland appears to value experience as an aid to spiritual progress, and behind the placing of the injunction to love in the mouth of Kynde may lie a feeling that the experience of passing through life towards death is a stimulus to love. This passage may be felt to conduce to patience, a virtue Langland connects with the growth of Charity.[51] Under the pressure of old age there is nothing for Will to do but suffer and trust in

[50] See Hugh White, 'Langland's Ymaginatif, Kynde and the *Benjamin Major*', *MAE*, 55 (1986), 241–8.
[51] The tree on which the fruit Charity grows is called 'Pacience . . . and pore symple of herte' at B XVI 8, for instance. See also C XV 274–8.

Kynde for his vengeance – the naturally inevitable progress through old age to death may be designed as a lesson in patience leading to love. Patience is a mortification of the demands of the self, a surrender of one's will to that of God (the character Patience offers *Fiat voluntas tua* as that by which one should live (B XIV 48–9)) and one can understand how the approaching dissolution of the self might make this surrender easier; easier too, perhaps, the giving of the self in love. In further explanation of Kynde's command of love one might suggest that Langland sees the approach to one's maker and judge – an approach all men naturally have to make – as conducive to the pursuit in general of virtue, which the poem now quite clearly understands to be the pursuit of love.

We might recall how at C X 168–9 Kynde is identified as love:

> . . . . Kynde, that alle kyne thynges wrouhte,
> The which is loue and lyf þat last withouten ende.

An association of Kynde with love is evident in all three major Kynde sequences. In Wit's speech in A and B, Kynde is *Anima*'s lover and looks to her welfare (the general identification of Kynde as love occurs in the C equivalent). In Passus B XI and XII Kynde's love is more extensive, covering all creatures and manifested particularly in the provision of the means of survival. In this episode Kynde also provides an incentive for man to love him in the signs of his power and love evident in the natural world. In Passus B XX the lesson of love is stated more explicitly and has a more general reference in that the object of the love taught does not now seem to be God alone. In this episode, furthermore, the lesson of love is more compelling – at least Will proceeds without demur to Unity where he is to learn the craft of love, rather than questioning the dispositions of Kynde as he does in B XI. The lesson is also more involving. It is no longer a matter of learning through observation, but through the living of one's *kynde* course. We might say that a *kynde* knowing regarding the necessity of loving has been achieved through experience, a knowing *kynde* both in the sense of 'proper' and of 'naturally derived'. We can say too that though it is hidden behind the menace of old age and death, Kynde's love for his creature man is apparent in the arranging of the course of life so that it inclines us to grow in virtue. We can also find a hint of that love in the suggestion that Kynde will indeed avenge the ravages of sin and death (B XX 204–5).

The presentation of Kynde, though he is always associated with love, differs markedly in the three major passages concerned with him. In the first he is responsible for establishing *Anima* in the Castle of *Caro* where she will be safe from the assaults of the *Princeps huius mundi*. Kynde appears as the protector of mankind. In the second episode Kynde is the sponsor of a system which includes the unreasonable sinfulness of man: he mysteriously permits a penetration by the forces of evil which in the earlier discourse of

Wit he was shown as attempting to prevent. Finally, Kynde actively leads the forces of physical destruction against man as a response to man's sinfulness. These changes of presentation may point to a growing realisation on Langland's part of the natural inevitability of exposure to the sin and suffering of this world and to a conviction of the desirability of this exposure for man's spiritual life.[52] It seems to be through the process of ageing and the suffering this involves (and here we might recall A XII) that Will comes to learn most compellingly of the need to love, and through his experience in the face of these things that he is stirred to enter Unity, the place where the lesson of love is to be learnt. The very unprotectedness of man from life in its physical aspect leads to the spiritual protection of Unity. Kynde gives permission to the forces of evil in this final episode too when he ceases from the work of destruction to see whether men will amend. It is clear that Kynde could, had he so wished, have destroyed the forces of Antichrist: he will, after all, finally destroy everything except Conscience (B XX 150–1). It may be that we should see Kynde as suffering here for some man's good as he does, according to Reason, in B XI (see 381). Conscience is perhaps the beneficiary in being forced out of Unity into active pursuit of Piers. Langland may see the life of virtue as in the last analysis one of continual pilgrimage rather than as a static occupation of a closed point of defence waiting for divine assistance. Pilgrimage suggests exposure to the chances of the world, and in this may lie some of its attractiveness for Langland. The pilgrim Patience is the apotheosis of openness to experience as he surrenders his own will and allows God's will to happen to him. We should remember that it is by association with Patience that Conscience is to become perfect.[53] The collapse of Unity seems to point to the sad inevitability of the failure of any structure in which men are involved to provide secure protection against the assaults of sin. Nevertheless, if the poem does in the end see the Christian life as pilgrimage and recognise exposure to the world as spiritually beneficial, then, insofar as being within Unity is to be closed off from the world, the collapse of Unity will not be entirely unfortunate. The Castle of

[52] In B XVIII Peace presents a rather different vindication of both suffering and the sin which is its cause:

> Forthi God, of his goodnesse, the firste gome Adam,
> Sette hym in solace and in sovereyn murthe;
> And siththe he suffred hym synne, sorwe to feele –
> To wite what wele was, kyndeliche to knowe it.
>
> (B XVIII 217–20)

See further the discussion in Chapter 4.

[53] According to Clergie at B XIII 214. In C Conscience says he will go with Patience 'parfitnesse to fynde' (C XV 184). Patience and openness to experience seem to be attributes of God himself. At B XI 379 Reason asks 'Who suffreth moore than God?', and B XVIII 217–24 speak of how 'God auntrede hymself and took Adames kynde' so that he could know what Adam suffered and find out what 'alle wo' is.

*Caro* and Unity are both enclosed places and image an insulation from life: it may be that we should find satisfaction in the poem's abandonment of them both.

The three pictures of Kynde successively presented may be assessed with reference to the principle of order, which is to view the sequence towards an increasing engagement with life under another aspect. Initially, Kynde is presented as the author of an harmonious order in which man enjoys a special resemblance to Him and as one who has provided for the spiritual welfare of man in this world. In contrast to this unproblematic picture, Passus B XI shows us man, as distinct from all the other inhabitants of the realm of *Myddelerthe*, out of harmony with Reason. The situation may remind us of that of which Nature complains in the *De Planctu Naturae*, but in *Piers Plowman* man's unreasonable behaviour is not viewed as a repudiation of Nature's rule, but takes place under the jurisdiction of Kynde who, we are assured, gives it permission for reasons not entirely clear to us. In his final appearance, Kynde is the inflicter of disease and death and even permits the collapse of Unity into which he has told Will to withdraw. We are explicitly informed that Kynde's last appearance in the world will be radically destructive (B XX 150–1). At the end of the poem we seem a long way from earlier Natures who bind the world in an ordered harmony and look to the preservation of life.[54]

Kynde comes to replace Truth as the designation of God the Father, Truth after B VII almost never being used as a name for God.[55] Interestingly, in B XVIII Truth, as one of the four daughters of God, is (with Righteousness) on the wrong side of the debate with Mercy and Peace; she thinks that man's sinfulness will prevent him being saved. It may be that Langland moves away from seeing the business of salvation in terms of the fulfilling of the demand to do well expressed in Truth's pardon and that as he alters his view on this, so his idea of the essential nature of God changes.[56] Truth as a name for God emphasises fulfilment of contract, judgement and justice.[57] As we have seen, Kynde is associated with love, and we shall see further that to be *kynde* is to be merciful.

---

[54] Kynde's destructiveness in the final sequence contrasts markedly with his concern for the continuation of life displayed earlier in the provision of livelihood for individual creatures and in education in procreation towards the preservation of species. The conflict between what seem to have been Kynde's earlier attitudes and his dismissal of the dreamer's worries over physical survival at B XX 209–11 is perhaps to be registered; the irony would provide added urgency and impetus to Kynde's assertion of the priority of the spiritual over the physical.

[55] At B IX 99, *Truth* seems to make better sense if understood to refer to true men rather than to God. At C X 181 where Pearsall reads 'of Treuthe' Skeat (his XI 181) has 'in treuthe'. (Pearsall's, of course, is not a full critical edition.) It is clear, anyway, that in the later stages of the poem the conception of God as Truth is not as prominent as it was earlier.

[56] This remains true even if we suppose that an attempt is made in Holy Church's discourse in Passus I to bring Truth and Love together. See discussion in Chapter 2.

[57] For a view similar to mine on the significance of the name Truth for God see Baker (1980).

In the one certain use of Truth to designate God after B VII, the Devil, just before the Harrowing of Hell, refers to Christ as Truth (B XVIII 294–5). The name Truth is particularly appropriate to Christ's dealings with the devils. In harrowing Hell, Christ will be meting out strict Old Testament justice. He informs Satan that

> the Olde Law graunteth
> That gilours be bigiled – and that is good reson:
> *Dentem pro dente et oculum pro oculo.*
> *Ergo* soule shal soule quyte and synne to synne wende,
> And al that man hath mysdo, I, man, wole amende it.
> Membre for membre [was amendes by the Olde Lawe],
> And lif for lif also – and by that lawe I clayme
> Adam and al his issue at my wille herafter. . . .
> So leve it noght, Lucifer, ayein the lawe I fecche hem,
> But by right and by reson raunsone here my liges:
> *Non veni solvere legem set adimplere.*
>
> (B XVIII 339–45; 349–50a)

Later Christ makes a distinction between the ways in which he will rule hell on the one hand and mankind on the other:

> my rightwisnesse and right shal rulen al helle,
> And mercy al mankynde bifore me in hevene.
>
> (B XVIII 397–8)

'Rightwisnesse and right' may well call forth the name Truth for God. But Righteousness was, with Truth, on the losing side of the argument between the four daughters of God about mankind's ultimate fate. As regards his dealings with man, God may seem more appropriately designated Kynde, since Kynde is associated with love and the name itself suggests benevolence.[58] Christ himself invokes the idea of *kynde*ness and the concept of kinship (*kyn* and *kynde* overlap semantically),[59] in justifying his mercy towards man:

> For I were an unkynde kyng but I my kyn helpe –
> And nameliche at swich a nede ther nedes help bihoveth:
> *Non intres in iudicium cum servo tuo.*
>
> (B XVIII 399–400a)

The Latin quotation points to God's setting aside strict justice in his dealings with mankind.

In addition, to call God Kynde suggests his accessibility to mankind, whereas the name Truth seems to set God beyond man's reach. Truth's injunction to do well, which surely has to be obeyed if one is to reach t/Truth, always encounters *nemo bonus*. Holy Church said that the true man was a god; if God is Kynde perhaps the *kynde* man is a god. But it may well be thought that it is easier to follow one's nature, and in this sense to be

---

[58] See discussion in Chapter 4.
[59] See *MED*, kinde n. 10. (c).

*kynde*, than it is to be true. Indeed the proposition *Nemo sine crimine vivit* arises out of the perception that men must some time follow their *kynde* (B XI 400–2). (We shall see in the next chapter that following one's flawed *kynde* so as simply to avoid *unkyndenesse* qualifies one for the mercy of God.) Even if one understands man's *kynde* as his true nature, the ideal pattern for his existence, rather than the corrupted actuality of his being, the demand that we should be *kynde* seems adapted to our capabilities. We are, after all, in some degree still partakers of our true nature.[60] We are *kynde* too in being creatures of the realm of Kynde. We might say that there is a naturalness to being *kynde* (the very meaning of the word enforces this idea) which, set together with the identification of God as Kynde, hints at what one might call a natural divinity in man.[61] That sense of a 'natural divinity' in man is called forth too by the treatment of *kynde*, which we shall consider in the next chapter.

Finally, one may suggest a relation between the three persons of the Trinity and the triad Dowel, Dobet and Dobest. God may be said to do well in his actions as Kynde the Creator, better in his actions as Christ the Redeemer and best in those as the Holy Spirit, in that, until the coming of Christ and then the Spirit, God's plan for history and his provision for the salvation of mankind have not reached their full development.[62] But besides this temporal sequence, the action of God in the here and now can be divided according to the persons of the Trinity. Thus Kynde has his particular operations to perform in the salvation history of the individual. B XI and B XX present two ways in which Kynde teaches man to love. Kynde's sphere of operation seems to be the natural experience of all men. As in the temporal sequence of the actions of the different persons of the Trinity so as regards the salvation of the contemporary individual the actions of Kynde may fall short of completeness. Though Will enters Unity as Kynde counsels and may even learn to love there, the collapse of Unity seems to indicate that 'natural' virtue is subject to decay, that security in the path to salvation

[60] The *imago Dei* which defines man's true nature has not been completely destroyed by the Fall. See, for example, Augustine's *De Spiritu et Littera* 28 (PL 44, 230f.).

[61] In line with this, there are suggestions that Langland believes that mere membership of the *kynde* man is enough for salvation. Christ says:

Ac my rightwisnesse and right shal rulen al helle,
And mercy al mankynde bifore me in hevene.
For I were an unkynde kyng but I my kyn helpe –

(B XVIII 397–9)

The suggestion is that Christ is obligated towards the *kynde* man by his kinship with it. The stress on kin relationship between Christ and man might be taken as another pointer to the 'natural divinity' of man. See Chapter 4, note 32.

[62] In Julian of Norwich too, there seems to be a sense that God's activity in *kynde* is completed by his activity in mercy and grace, activities associated with Christ and the Holy Spirit respectively.

requires the presence of Piers, who perhaps at this stage figures Christ,[63] and Grace.

But the collapse of Unity may, as we have seen, be permitted for the ultimate good of man. Insofar as the collapse states a general truth about man's natural condition, it may be that that condition is paradoxically vindicated. And the figure of Conscience seems to permit some optimism about the natural capacities of man. He goes on seeking the good, as his search for Piers at the end of the poem shows, and we are told that Kynde will not at the last destroy this faculty, which thus appears as quintessentially natural to man.[64] But optimistic suggestions about man's natural condition

---

[63] On this see, for example, Schmidt (1987) on XX 381, p. 357.

[64] Certain other passages speak of a personified Kynde. Of the crucified Christ we are told:

> Ac was no boy so boold Goddes body to touche;
> For he was knyght and kynges sone, Kynde foryaf that throwe
> That noon harlot were so hardy to leyen hond upon hym.
>
> (B XVIII 75–7)

One wonders why Kynde features here; God's creativity does not seem to be in point. It may be that Langland thought that the jurisdiction of Kynde over the processes of this world extended to the social order. Kynde may preside over an order of the naturally appropriate in the social and other realms, and what he is said to prohibit here may be a violation of the naturally appropriate: it is more fitting that Longeus, a knight, should pierce Christ's side. In the following passage, it seems rather difficult to take *kynde* as God. Patience imagines the poor man claiming joy of God and saying:

> "Lo! briddes and beestes, that no blisse ne knoweth,
> And wilde wormes in wodes, thorugh wyntres thow hem grevest,
> And makest hem wel neigh meke and mylde for defaute,
> And after thow sendest hem somer, that is hir sovereyn joye,
> And blisse to alle that ben, bothe wilde and tame."
> Thanne may beggeris, as beestes, after boote waiten,
> That al hir lif han lyved in langour and in defaute.
> But God sente hem som tyme som manere joye
> Outher here or elliswhere, kynde wolde it nevere;
> For to wrotherhele was he wroght that nevere was joye shapen!
>
> (B XIV 111–20)

Schmidt, 1987, p. 167, glosses 'kynde wolde it nevere' '. . . . would be a contradiction to their very nature', but it does not seem to be the natures of individual things that are displayed in the preceding talk of the animal kingdom to which the *kynde* clause appears to have reference. What Langland seems to be suggesting is that the animal world displays a principle which binds God in his dealings with men. This principle is, of course, one which God has set up for himself, so that the appearance of opposition between God and *kynde* is somewhat misleading. The precise meaning of *kynde* is difficult to ascertain. We might gloss it 'the principle according to which the world is arranged, evident in the animal creation' and relate this *kynde* to the Kynde of B XI. We might note how, as in B XI, an inspection of the animal world, the world of *kynde*, seems to provide grounds for a deduction as to the nature of God and to reveal his love. (Perhaps because Langland felt the difficulties arising from the reference to *kynde* here, C XV 298 substitutes 'ellis hit were reuthe' for 'kynde wolde it nevere.') Similarly, at B XX 253–6a we find a use of Kynde which seems best understood in terms of the gloss just offered:

> And if ye coveite cure, Kynde wol yow telle
> That in mesure God made alle manere thynges,
> And sette it at a certein and at a siker nombre,

and capacities are only to be expected in a poem in which the figure who superintends the natural is securely identified as God in a term which points to his benevolence and love.

---

> And nempnede hem names newe, and noumbrede the sterres:
> *Qui numerat multitudinem stellarum et omnibus eis &c.*

In the following too, *kynde* appears as a force not to be identified with God:

> And Mede is manered after hym [her father Fals], right as [asketh kynde]:
> *Qualis pater, talis filius. Bona arbor bonum fructum facit.*

> (B II 27–27a)

C reads

> And Mede is manered aftur hym, as men of kynde carpeth:
> *Talis pater, talis filia.*

> (C II 27–27a)

Pearsall, 1987, glosses 'of kynde' 'concerning kinship'. Schmidt, 1987, gives 'nature requires' for 'asketh kynde'. In both texts either of these suggested meanings seems possible. If Schmidt is followed, *kynde* will mean general Nature; reference to God is unnecessary and inappropriate for this well-known natural principle. See also C X 241–2a where *kynde* probably refers to species of things.

# Chapter Four

# *Being Kynde*

Since Langland has seen fit to call God Kynde, it is no surprise to find that he attaches great importance to men being *kynde* and that *unkyndenesse* is a particularly heinous sin in his scheme of things. But it is also true that Langland understands *kynde* to have certain negative aspects which pull man away from the path of virtue. This seems to be part of Langland's awareness, an awareness I have suggested grows with the poem, that the natural cannot be aligned with the good unproblematically. It is this darker side of *kynde* which I want first to consider.

We have already seen in discussing *kynde wit* that Langland is prepared to make derogatory comments about the law of *kynde*; adherence to Mahomet was condemned in the following terms:

> A man þat hihte Makameth for Messie they hym holdeth
> And aftur his leryng they lyue and by lawe of kynde,
> And when kynde hath his cours and no contrarie fyndeth
> Thenne is lawe ylefte and leute vnknowe.
> *Beaute sanz bounte* blessed was hit neuere
> Ne kynde *sanz cortesie* in no contreye is preysed.

(C XVII 159–64)

The idea of the law of *kynde* may be equivocal here: Langland seems to use it initially to refer to the natural moral law, but then slips into treating it as the order of natural impulses, for the natural moral law needs no 'contrarie'. Natural impulse, then, needs to be restrained if law and *leute* are to be preserved, and in this way the *kynde* is a threat to right action.[1]

---

[1] There is an important division in medieval understandings of the law of nature between those that relate it to man's reason and those that relate it to the urges that man shares with the animals (on this see, e.g., Tierney (1963), and W. Onclin, 'Le droit naturel selon les romanistes des XIIe et XIIIe siècles', in *Miscellanea Moralia in honorem eximii domini Arthur Janssen* Vol. 2, pp. 329–37 (Louvain/Gembloux, 1949)). When it is taken in this second sense, the law of nature can easily become something threatening the morality of an individual's actions. Chaucer and Gower's understanding of the natural seems to me deeply affected by a worry that the natural is not a force necessarily aligned with Reason. Gower, who habitually sees the natural in terms of the animal, would have sympathised much with the notion that the natural

At the beginning of Passus B XX Nede appeals to the *lawe of kynde* to justify theft in cases of extreme need. He asks the indigent Will whether he could not have stolen and excused himself on the grounds that

> nede ne hath no lawe, ne nevere shal falle in dette
> For thre thynges he taketh his lif for to save? –
> That is, mete whan man hym werneth, and he no moneye weldeth,
> Ne wight noon wol ben his borugh, ne wed hath noon to legge;
> And he ca[cch]e in that caas and come therto by sleighte,
> He synneth noght, soothliche, that so wynneth his foode.
> And though he come so to a clooth, and kan no bettre chevyssaunce,
> Nede anoon righte nymeth hym under maynprise.
> And if hym list for to lape, the iawe of kynde wolde
> That he dronke at ech dych, er he [deide for thurst].

(B XX 10–19)

There is orthodox support for Nede's assertion of the legitimacy of theft *in extremis*,[2] but it seems very likely that Nede here is an evil tempter, the forerunner of Antichrist, and that his persuasions are to be rejected.[3] It is not altogether clear whether the reference is to the natural moral law or to the order of natural impulsive urges, but it may well be that we have here another instance of the treacherousness of unrestrained natural impulse.[4]

---

needs to be restrained (see, e.g., *Confessio Amantis* VII 5372–81), though the sphere in which he feels this need is that of sexual love, whereas elsewhere a natural morality based on impulses that man shares with the animals seems satisfactory. Langland, though he recognises this problem over the natural, seems to be able to find an accommodation of the natural within a moral framework which Chaucer and Gower cannot in the end make, much as they seem interested in so doing. See Conclusion.

[2] See, for example, Aquinas, *Summa Theologica* II IIae q. 66 a. 7. Dunning (1980), p. 21, says that the medieval theologians taught that in extreme need a man had a duty, under pain of sin, to take the necessaries of life wherever he could find them. This assertion is not documented from the theologians, and it may only be the weaker proposition that a man in extreme need is entitled to the necessaries of life and may disregard the normal property rights of others to get them that the theologians set out. On this see Carlyle (1903–36), V pp. 18–19 and II p. 142.

[3] See the important discussion of Nede by Robert Adams, 'The Nature of Need in "Piers Plowman" XX', *Traditio*, 34 (1978), 272–302. Bloomfield (1961), pp. 135–43, sees Nede as an agent of good, as do Robertson and Huppé (195). See also Baldwin (1981), p. 9. Schmidt (1987), registers no disquiet about Nede, but Pearsall (1978), on C XXII 37, p. 363, suggests that Nede's advice is not in line with what we have been told about God's provisions for the faithful. Patience, a figure of considerable authority, says that one should not worry about the 'necessaries' of life even in the face of starvation (B XIV 50–9a), though see Martin (1979), as cited in Chapter 1, note 78. See also Pamela Gradon, 'Langland and the Ideology of Dissent', *Proceedings of the British Academy*, 66 (1980), 179–205 (p. 203).

[4] Schmidt (1987), p. 356, comments *'the lawe of kynde* here means less *lex naturalis*, "natural law", the principle of (moral) conduct forming part of man's nature as created by God, than "the instinct of self-preservation" (also ordained by God and prior to and, in some circumstances, superior to any other man made *lex*)'. Schmidt's 'less . . . than' indicates that he finds a certain ambivalence in the phrase *lawe of kynde*. I would be inclined to associate it with the automatic motions of man (this would be congruent with the use of the idea of the law of *kynde* in the C XVII 159–64 passage discussed above). Nede, though, is invoking the term because it has moral weight in justifying (not merely excusing) the course of action he advocates.

Whatever *lawe of kynde* means, its credentials as a moral guide will not be strengthened if Nede is indeed evil.

On several occasions Langland associates *kynde* with the flesh, and the opprobrium frequently visited upon that entity in medieval writings falls upon *kynde*.[5] In the following passage, at least *kynde* and the flesh do not seem positively sinful:

> Wedewes and wedewares, þat here ownere wil forsaken
> And chaste leden here lyf, is lyf of contemplacioun,
> And more lykynde to oure lorde then lyue as kynde asketh
> And folewe þat the flesche wole and fruyt forth brynge,
> That *Actiua* lyf lettred men in here langage hit calleth.
>
> (C XVIII 76–80)

But the *kynde* does clearly prompt to sin according to Lady Mede:

> . . . . I wolde noght spare
> For to be youre frend, frere, and faile yow nevere
> While ye love lordes that lecherie haunten
> And lakketh noght ladies that loven wel the same.
> It is a freletee of flessh – ye fynden it in bokes –
> And a cours of kynde, wherof we comen alle.
> Who may scape the sclaundre, the scathe is soone amended;
> It is synne of the sevene sonnest relessed.
>
> (B III 51–8)

Though Lady Mede is plainly wrong to encourage laxity towards lechery, her view that it is the least of the seven deadly sins may be admissible.[6] But, even if this is so, we would do well to pause before allowing *kynde* to be so compromisingly implicated in the frailty of the flesh on the evidence of a witness plainly concerned to scrape up as much respectability as possible, however spurious, for lechery. In fact, though, characters of unimpeachable authority seem to understand the relation of *kynde* to the flesh very much as does Mede. When Reason says that man must suffer *wo*

> In fondynge of the flessh and of the fend bothe.
> For man was maad of swich a matere he may noght wel asterte
> That som tyme hym bitit to folwen his kynde.
> Caton acordeth therwith – *Nemo sine crimine vivit!*
>
> (B XI 399–402)

---

[5] Writers of homily contemporary with Langland, wishing to see the natural as right and proper, tend to avoid an association of the *kynde* with the morally dubious flesh.

[6] See Pearsall's note on C III 59–62, p. 68. On the other hand lechery is felt to be particularly abhorrent in some medieval writings. See, for instance, *The Tretyse of Loue*, ed. John H. Fisher, *EETS* o.s. 223 (London, 1951), pp. 101–2. Consider also the following passage from *Select English Works of John Wyclif*, ed. T. Arnold (Oxford, 1869–71), II p. 276:

> Poul biddiþ here to trewe men, *þat no man bigile hem in bileve bi veyn wordis* which þei speken, þat þes ben no synnes or liȝt; as lecherie is kyndeli, as þei seien, . . . . Siche veyn wordis þat excusen synne done myche harme among men, . . .

it does seem to be implied that the naturalness of the sins of the flesh constitutes an excuse for them.[7] And the implication that man can enter a legitimate plea in mitigation for certain sins because the *matere* of which he is made inclines him towards them is made explicit in the following speech of the Samaritan, a higher authority still than Reason, in which *kynde*, sin and flesh are again linked:

> The wif is oure wikked flessh that wol noght be chastised,
> For kynde clyveth on hym evere to contrarie the soule.
> And though it falle, it fynt skiles, that "Frelete it made,"
> And "That is lightly foryyven and foryeten bothe
> To man that mercy asketh and amende thenketh."

(B XVII 331–5)

The threat to the *kynde* involved in the repeated recognition that the natural impulses are treacherous for the man who would live the life of virtue here seems to be defused by the suggestion that the *kynde* sins of the flesh do not really much matter (given repentance on the part of the sinner). As we shall see, this suggestion accords very well with the general drift of the Samaritan's discourse.

It would accord well too, of course, with a general desire on Langland's part to see the natural as a force for good, as would the fact that Langland much more frequently treats the *kynde* as morally positive than he finds it conducing to evil. The law of *kynde* may on occasion seem questionable in its authority or influence, but Langland is also able to understand it as urging to the good. So we find the following exhortation regarding those who have suffered at the hands of Fortune or false men:

> Conforte hem with thi catel for Cristes love of hevene;
> Love hem and lene hem, for so lawe of [kynde wolde]:
> *Alter alterius onera portate.*

(B VI 220–1a)

The text here is from *Galatians* 6, 2 which speaks of bearing one another's burdens as following the law of Christ. Langland seems to have identified the law of Christ with the law of nature in a way that is perfectly orthodox,[8] but which accords a very high status to the law of nature, and which, again, would be in line with a desire to find the natural a power for good.

The high moral status of being *kynde*, according to Wit, is apparent when he tells Will

---

[7] Gower likewise finds mitigation for sexual behaviour which is against reason in the strength of the natural urges to which man is subject (see *Confessio Amantis* III 384–91, 1193–9). For Langland's tolerance towards the flesh see M. T. Tavormina, ' "Bothe two ben goode": Marriage and Virginity in *Piers Plowman* C 18. 68–100.', *JEGP* 81 (1982), 320–30.

[8] See chapter 1, note 19.

## Being Kynde

> · dobest out of dobet & dowel gynneþ springe
> Among men of þis molde þat mek ben & kynde.

(A X 127–8)

Being *kynde* here is certainly a requirement for *dobest*, and perhaps for *dowel* and *dobet* also. But this passage also raises a question about the meaning of the adjective *kynde* as Langland uses it. Rather than attaching to the idea of the natural, might it not simply bear its modern meaning?[9] This issue over the meaning of *kynde* must now be addressed.

The question I have just put has been asked and answered variously of the *kynde* in the following passage. Scripture is telling Will that Christians need more than baptism to attain salvation:

> Ac Cristene men withoute moore maye noght come to hevene,
> For that Crist for Cristene men deide, and confermed the lawe
> That whoso wolde and wilneth with Crist to arise –
> *Si cum Christo surrexistis &c* –
> He sholde lovye and lene and the lawe fulfille.
> That is, love thi Lord God levest aboven alle,
> And after, alle Cristene creatures in commune, ech man oother;
> And thus bilongeth to lovye, that leveth to be saved.
> And but we do thus in dede er the day of dome,
> It shal bisitten us ful soure, the silver that we kepen,
> And oure bakkes that mothe-eten be, and seen beggeris go naked,
> Or delit in wyn and wildefowel, and wite any in defaute.
> For every Cristene creature sholde be kynde til oother,
> And sithen hethen to helpe in hope of amendement.

(B X 349–61)

C. S. Lewis supposes that *kynde* here bears its modern meaning, but Ida Gordon disagrees and argues that at this period *kynde* and related adjectives and adverbs always have some attachment to the sense 'natural'.[10] In this particular instance we could suggest a confined reference of the natural to the nature of Christians – it is part of the nature of the Christian to be charitable – or see *kynde* as referring more embracingly to the nature of man in general, or to the law of nature.[11] It is worth noting that what is involved in being *kynde* is loving and giving, activity dictated by the law of *kynde* in the passage discussed earlier, where the reference to the natural is not in doubt. I am inclined to support Gordon's reading of this particular passage and also her general point about usage at this period. It is certainly very difficult to be sure that the sense natural is not relevant in usages of *kynde* as

---

[9] The first citation for the modern meaning in MED is dated to before 1333. But there must be a considerable degree of uncertainty as to just when this meaning ceases to have any association with the idea of the natural.

[10] Ida Gordon, *The Double Sorrow of Troilus* (Oxford, 1970), pp. 145–50.

[11] The law of nature can be defined with reference to the nature of man. For an account of how this is so in Aquinas see F. C. Copleston, *Aquinas* (Harmondsworth, 1955), pp. 221ff.

an adjective in much of the homiletic literature of the period;[12] the fact that *kynde* can still be used to mean natural in the later fourteenth century makes it likely that even where the modern meaning of *kynde* is appropriate the sense 'natural' would also have been felt, and this likelihood is further increased by the naturalness of beneficence according to the deep-rooted Christian realist tradition: man's (true) nature is, for this way of thinking, good and loving. The law of nature, furthermore, requires love. In Langland's case we shall find instances in which *kynde* terms for which a modern meaning is appropriate are used in close proximity to *kynde* terms which certainly refer to the idea of nature, and since Langland has a great propensity for word-play it seems likely, at least in these instances, that the modern meaning is not the only one carried. But for some passages in which *kynde* terms appear the case for a meaning attached to the idea of the natural may rest largely on the general considerations I have just outlined. This is perhaps so in the following passage, though we might note that the *unkynde* will is evidently an unloving one, and recall that love at least for the needy, and a preparedness to carry another's burden are recognised as dictates of the law of *kynde* at B VI 220–1a. The passage speaks of Judas:

> Thanne wente forth that wikked man and with the Jewes mette,
> And tolde hem a tokne how to knowe with Jesus,
> The which tokne to this day to muche is yused –
> That is, kissynge and fair countenaunce and unkynde wille.
>
> (B XVI 146–9)

Again, the suggestion at B VI 220–1a that it is naturally incumbent upon one to love and give to those in need makes one feel less hesitation than one might, if one were working only on a general sense that a *kynde* term is likely to relate to the idea of the natural, in understanding the *kyndenesse* of the following passage with reference to the natural. Sloth is confessing:

> If any man dooth me a bienfait or helpeth me at nede,
> I am unkynde ayeins his curteisie and kan nought understonden it;
> For I have and have had somdel haukes maneres –
> I am noght lured with love but ther ligge aught under the thombe.
> The kyndenesse that myn evenecristene kidde me fernyere
> Sixty sithes I, Sleuthe, have foryete it siththe
> In speche and in sparyng of speche;
>
> (B V 430–6)

---

[12] Take, for instance, the following passage from the Arnold collection of Wycliffite writings (II 336):

> Poul moveþ in þis epistle, for former kyndenes of Crist, to be kynde to him aȝen. For clerkis seien, and soiþ it is, þat boþe God and kynde haten þat a man dwelle unkynde after greet kyndenesse þat he haþ taken.

Whilst we might gloss *kyndenes(se)* 'benevolence' or 'kind deed', and whilst *unkynde* has the sense 'ungrateful', the reference to the entity *kynde* makes it very difficult to sustain any claim that there is no sense of 'natural' present in these terms.

A *kyndenesse* here seems equivalent to a *bienfait*, and if we do see a connection with the natural here, it will appear that acts of generosity and love are in some sense natural to man. Different senses are possible for the *unkynde* of the second line. It might refer to a failure to be generous and benevolent as men naturally should be or it might mean 'ungrateful'. 'Ungrateful' is a fairly common meaning of *unkynde* in Middle English:[13] Gower uses *unkindeshipe* for the Latin *ingratitudo*, and the manner in which he speaks of being *unkinde* in the sense of ungrateful as *ayein kinde* suggests that for him the *kinde* element of *unkindeshipe*, even when this means ingratitude, retains its attachment to the idea of the natural.[14] In either case, Sloth's omission can be taken as a falling off from what is natural, and we should probably not seek to confine the *kynde* to just one of the possible meanings.

There is another potential difficulty over meaning. In the passage on which Lewis and Gordon differ, I suggested that *kynde*, if understood in Gordon's way, might be taken to have a restricted reference to the nature of Christians in particular rather than the nature of man in general or to the law of nature. But here again, as with the modern sense of *kynde* and the meaning 'natural', it may be difficult to maintain strict separation of meaning; at least it will be difficult to justify a restriction of reference in the B V 430–6 passage since Langland has told us that the law of *kynde* – a general law – requires one to help one's fellow-men. As for *kynde*, so, I think, for *unkynde*, where there exists the possibility that the nature referred to is that of the Christian in particular, as is the case in several stigmatisations as *unkynde*. *Anima*, for instance, tells us that

> In savacion of the feith Seint Thomas was ymartired:
> Amonges unkynde Cristene for Cristes love he deyede
>
> (B XV 521–2)

If one wished to relate *unkynde* here to the nature of the Christian *qua* Christian one could see the unnaturalness involved as a matter of Christians failing to stand by Christ or of showing hostility to a fellow-Christian. This is readily understandable as against the (true) nature of Christians. But it is equally possible to give *unkynde* a more general reference; the unnaturalness may lie in the committing of murder, which we shall see is later said to be *unkynde*. Alternatively, or additionally, one might understand *unkynde* as 'ungrateful'. One is entitled, I think, to understand the *unkynde* Christians

---

[13] See OED, Unkind 3a.
[14] See *Confessio Amantis* V 4923–4:

> It is al on to seie unkinde
> As thing which don is ayein kinde,

and the marginal gloss at the head of the section from which this passage comes (V vii).

who martyr Thomas to be unnatural *qua* men, and I shall take this to be so in similar cases also.

Again, it is probably inappropriate and unnecessary to restrict the reference of *unkynde* to the nature of neighbours when Piers speaks as follows of the devil's assault on the Tree of Charity:

> And thanne fondeth the fend my fruyt to destruye
> With alle the wiles that he kan, and waggeth the roote,
> And casteth up to the crop unkynde neighebores,
> Bakbiteris brewecheste, brawleris and chideris, . . . .

(B XVI 40–3)

Though it is the (true) nature of a neighbour, as we know from the parable of the Good Samaritan, to offer assistance rather than hostility, it is pretty clear that this behaviour from anyone, neighbour or not, is hardly in the spirit of bearing one another's burden, and hence may reasonably be condemned as against the law of nature. The *unkynde*ness involved may, in fact, be taken as a quite general one, relating to something in the basic constitution or awareness of all men.

These observations do not quite make an end of semantic difficulties. In the following passage *unkyndely* is used to signify a breach of the natural and proper order regarding marriage:

> For some, as I se now, sooth for to telle,
> For coveitise of catel unkyndely ben wedded.

(B IX 156–7)

A modern sense for *unkyndely* does not seem possible here, but quite what the unnaturalness referred to is not clear. Langland may think that marrying for money is itself unnatural,[15] but other possibilities are suggested in the continuation of the passage. The point may be that natural marriages are made for love:

> For no londes, but for love, loke ye be wedded, . . . .

(B IX 177)

or a breach of the principle 'like to like' may constitute the unnaturalness,[16] the typical marriage for money, it seems, involving a disparity in the partners' age:

> It is an uncomly couple, by Christ! as me thynketh –
> To yeven a yong wenche to an [y]olde feble, . . . .

(B IX 162–3)

[15] Langland, no doubt encouraged by the alliterative possibilities, frequently links covetousness and *unkynde*ness. But the connection is not merely a matter of metrical convenience. Covetousness is opposed to giving, which is an outward sign of love towards one's fellow men, and failure to give and to love are central in Langland's conception of *unkynde*ness. We shall find the allegorical figures Coveitise and Unkyndenesse paired as two particularly significant opponents of the good elsewhere in the poem. Coveitise is actually accused of *unkynde*ness by Repentance at B V 269.

[16] For the principle of like to like as a condition of proper marriage see also in this passage line 160.

Again, the ensuing lines perhaps make the possibility of procreation a requirement of the natural marriage:

> Or wedden any wodewe for welthe of hir goodes
> That nevere shal barn bere but if it be in armes!
>
> (B IX 164–5)

The precise grounds of its use perhaps cannot be determined, but the *unkyndely* represents a strong moral disapproval – in fact this is its prime function, rather than to introduce consideration of exactly what is unnatural in marriage.

In the following passage, too, there is some doubt as to what *unkyndenesse* involves:

> And if men lyvede as mesure wolde, sholde nevere moore be defaute
> Amonges Cristene creatures, if Cristes wordes ben trewe.
> Ac unkyndenesse *caristiam* maketh amonges Cristen peple,
> And over-plentee maketh pryde amonges poore and riche;
> Ac mesure is so muche worth it may noght be to deere;
>
> (B XIV 70–4)

The first two lines here suggest that the *unkyndenesse* of the third involves lack of measure in consumption. That would be quite in keeping with traditional thinking about the natural, and Langland himself invokes the idea of nature as the proper measure of consumption (admittedly in quotation) at Passus B XV 342e:

> *Porro non indiget monachus, si habeat quod nature sufficit.* [17]

But it is possible that an ellipsis of logic occurs, and that the *unkyndenesse* refers to a failure of generosity among those who have more than they need to live in accordance with the principle of measure. Or perhaps both meanings should be admitted – after all, not being content with enough is liable to make people ungenerous.

We can now return to an examination of Langland's deployment of *kynde* and *unkynde*. It is, of course, absolutely standard for medieval writers to condemn *unkyndenesse* and to censure various kinds of behaviour as *unkynde*.[18] But one should mark the high status Langland accords *unkynde-*

---

[17] When Glotoun says that he has

> ouer-sopped at my soper and som tyme at nones
> More then my kynde myhte deffye, . . . .
>
> (C VI 429–30)

the *kynde*, though it seems to refer to the physical system of an individual (cp. *Confessio Amantis* II 3119–25; IV 3303–5; VI 657–64), also probably bears moral weight.

[18] Two examples from the Arnold collection of Wycliffite writings: when a man is 'wraþþid wiþouten resoun', his anger is 'unkyndely venym aȝen þe state of innocence' (I 16); the sin of Sodom is 'more unkyndely þen any oþer lecchorye' (III 162).

*nesse* in the pantheon of Vice. It is a status it shares with *coveitise*. *Unkyndenesse* and *coveitise* are specified as the allegorical country through which Conscience and Patience may have to pass as they go on their pilgrimage; no other sins are mentioned:

> Thanne hadde Pacience, as pilgrymes han, in his poke vitailles:
> Sobretee and symple speche and soothfast bileve,
> To conforte hym and Conscience if thei come in place
> There unkyndenesse and coveitise is, hungry contrees bothe.
>
> (B XIII 216–19)

The two vices are second only to Pride in Grace's picture of the dispensation of Antichrist:

> And thanne shal Pride be Pope and prynce of Holy Chirche,
> Coveitise and Unkyndenesse Cardinals hym to lede.
>
> (B XIX 224–5)

and, indeed, in Antichrist's siege of Unity, the two are found ranged against Conscience:

> Envye herfore hatede Conscience,
> And freres to philosophie he fond hem to scole,
> The while Coveitise and Unkyndenesse Conscience assaillede.
>
> (B XX 295–7)

Perhaps more tellingly still, in a passage to which we shall return (B XVII 205ff.), the Samaritan says that the two are able to quench God's mercy. Clearly Langland has considerable respect for the destructive talents of this pair.

The insistent association of *unkyndenesse* with *coveitise* points, I think, to what for Langland is central in the idea of *kynde*ness. *Coveitise* is a force in opposition to giving, and giving is the practical expression of love – 'Love hem and lene hem'. The elevated position among the vices enjoyed both by *coveitise* and *unkyndenesse* is the result of their striking out directly against Love itself.

In several passages *kyndenesse* and *unkyndenesse* are presented in terms of a preparedness to give, or the reverse. One might instance B V 430–6 and B X 349–61 of the passages quoted above, and suggest that context indicates fairly certainly that failure to give is central also to the *unkyndenesse* of B XIII 216–19 and of B XIV 70–4 (the association of Unkyndenesse and Coveitise elsewhere points in the same direction). In the following passage, the context again suggests that the *unkyndenesse* which replaces *kyndenesse* is a grasping unwillingness to part charitably with one's wealth:

> Mede of mysdoeris makiþ hem so riche
> Þat lawe is lord waxen & leute is pore,
> Vnkyndenesse is comaund*our*, & kyndenesse is banisshit.
>
> (A III 272–4)

The involvement of the idea of the *kynde* with giving permits the usage *'kynde of'* and *'unkynde of'*:

> Allas that a Cristene creature shal be unkynde til another!
> Syn Jewes, that we jugge Judas felawes,
> Eyther helpeth oother of that that hym nedeth.
> Whi nel we Cristene of Cristes good [as kynde be]
> As Jewes, that ben oure loresmen? Shame to us alle!
> The commune for hir unkyndenesse, I drede me, shul abye.
>
> (B IX 84–9)

The following passage bears considerable resemblances to that at B VI 220-1a in which the law of *kynde* demanded that one should love the needy and give to them.[19]

> Forthi love we as leve children shal, and ech man laughe of oother,
> And of that ech man may forbere, amende there it nedeth,
> And every man helpe oother – for hennes shul we alle:
> *Alter alterius onera portate*
> And be we noght unkynde of oure catel, ne of oure konnyng neither,
> For woot no man how neigh it is to ben ynome fro bothe.
>
> (B XI 208–12)

Sometimes covetousness is explicitly opposed to *kynde*ness:

> Let not þi left hond, late ne raþe,
> Be war what þi riȝt hond werchiþ or deliþ,
> A[c] so preuyliche parte it þat pride be not seiȝe,
> Neiþer in siȝt ne in þi soule, for god hymself knowiþ
> Who is curteis or kynde or coueitous, or ellis.
>
> (A III 55–9)

Haukyn says of himself:

> So if I kidde any kyndenesse myn evencristen to helpe,
> Upon a cruwel coveitise my conscience gan hange.
>
> (B XIII 389–90)

Patience has seen that Haukyn's coat

> of pointes . . . .
> Was colomy thorugh coveitise and unkynde desiryng.
> More to good than to God the gome his love caste, . . . .
>
> (B XIII 354–6)

It is possible that *coveitise* and *unkynde desiryng* here are one and the same thing, since there follows an extended description of the ways in which Haukyn has attempted to satisfy his covetousness, without reference to any other sort of sin. Certainly his *unkynde*ness towards kith and kin is very much bound up with covetousness in the following passage:

---

[19] On the issue of meaning, Langland's earlier association of this text with the law of *kynde* suggests that here too the *unkynde* should be understood with reference to the natural.

> And whoso borwed of me aboughte the tyme
> With presentes pryvely, or paide som certeyn –
> So wolde he or noght wolde he, wynnen I wolde;
> And bothe to kith and to kyn unkynde of that ich hadde.
>
> (B XIII 375–8)

These connections between *unkyndenesse* and covetousness make one wonder whether the *unkynde werkes* of the following passage should be associated particularly with an unwillingness to give. Patience is explaining to Haukyn how his sin-befouled coat can be kept clean:

> And Dobest kepe[th] clene from unkynde werkes.
> Shal nevere my[te] bymolen it, ne mothe after biten it,
> Ne fend ne fals man defoulen it in thi lyve.
>
> (B XIV 22–4)

Perhaps we should understand Dobest here with reference to Patience's radical anti-materialism. For Patience goes on to suggest that one should not worry about material things, even if

> nevere greyn growed, ne grape upon vyne, . . . .
>
> (B XIV 31)

and claims to have sufficient *liflode* in 'a pece of the Paternoster – *Fiat voluntas tua*' (B XIV 48–9). It is in this anti-materialist stance that Patience's challenge to Haukyn lies.[20] Patience is confronting Haukyn as a representative of a life centred on food-production, a life organised round Piers earlier in the poem (Haukyn associates himself with Piers at B XIII 224–40). We have seen that that life is open to the charge of over-accommodating the material, and we can suggest further that its concern with the material gives an opening to covetousness. Patience's role as the incarnation of anti-materialism might indicate that the *unkynde* works he has in mind spring from covetousness, which results in an unpreparedness to be *kynde* of one's possessions.[21]

Alternatively, the *unkynde werkes* here could be taken quite generally as co-extensive with sin.[22] Certainly the passage accords high status in the

[20] This remains so, even if we accept that Patience is forced away from the full radicalness of his anti-materialist stance because of Langland's suspiciousness of idealising absolutes, as Martin (1979), pp. 135ff., suggests.

[21] There might also be present in *unkynde* a sense that the requirements of nature are over-supplied by the covetous man; he goes beyond the satisfaction of natural needs and desires.

[22] The possibility arises because of the availability of an ultimately neo-platonic view on nature and sin according to which a nature, as Augustine has it, *in quantum natura est, bona est*. In the following passage Augustine puts the matter explicitly:

> Si ergo malo illo adempto manet natura purgatior, bono autem detracto non manet ulla natura: hoc ibi facit naturam quod bonum habet; quod autem malum, non natura, sed contra naturam est.
>
> (*Contra Epistolam Manichaei* I 33; PL 42, 199)

We might also note the following remark from the Arnold collection of Wycliffite writings (I 371):

> Whanne a man synneþ aȝens God, and mote nede be ponished of him, þis is oon unkindeli drede, as it is unkindeli to synne;

realm of evil to the *unkynde*. That status is fully recognised in the Samaritan's speech at the end of Passus B XVII. There *unkyndenesse* involves a failure to assimilate oneself to the nature of the Holy Ghost as Mercy. To be *unkynde*, in fact, is to be opposed to the nature of God – and this would provide strong justification for taking the *unkynde werkes* of which Patience speaks to be sin in general. But the Samaritan's *unkyndenesse* seems to be more confined than this; the opposition to the mercy of God is expressed in a failure to give charitably and in murder, and against this *unkyndenesse* may be set sins we might wish to call *kynde*, because they seem to be engrained in our nature, or to be the products of the natural conditions of our existence. It is possible to understand *kyndenesse* and *unkyndenesse* with reference to an ideal, unfallen nature, so that sin in general can be considered unnatural, but (whatever may be the case with *unkynde werkes*) in the end, Langland seems to want to tie his concept of the *kynde* to what is natural here and now, and to find that, fallen as it is, essentially good. This positive attitude has much to do, I think, with Christ's assumption of human nature, but before we turn to that we should make a detailed examination of what the Samaritan says.

The thesis of the passage is that the Holy Ghost will fail to blaze, that is, to express His true nature as Mercy, to those who show unmerciful *unkynde*ness towards their fellow men, in not alleviating need (we remember how this is dictated by the law of *kynde*) or in committing murder. This is unfolded over a considerable length of text, but the first mention of *unkynde*ness gives us much of the message:

> And as thow seest som tyme sodeynliche a torche –
> The blase therof yblowe out, yet brenneth the weke –
> Withouten leye or light, that [lowe] the macche brenneth;
> So is the Holy Goost God, and grace withoute mercy
> To alle unkynde creatures that coveite to destruye
> Lele love or lif that Oure Lord shapte.

> (B XVII 214–19)

The opposition of *unkyndenesse* to the quintessential Christian virtue of love is immediately apparent. It is an opposition entirely expected from what we have seen of *kyndenesse* and *unkyndenesse* thus far. The very meaning of the word sets *unkyndenesse* against love. Here, though, the hostility is made utterly explicit by having the *unkynde* positively desiring to destroy love.[23] Langland goes on to explain exactly why the Holy Ghost does not show His mercy to these *unkynde creatures*:

> And as glowynge gledes gladeth noght thise werkmen
> That werchen and waken in wyntres nyghtes,
> As dooth a kex or a candle that caught hath fir and blaseth,

---

[23] C XIX 181, however, substitutes *lycame* for *love*.

> Namoore dooth Sire ne Sone ne Seint Spirit togideres
> Graunte no grace ne forgifnesse of synnes
> Til the Holy Goost gynne to glowe and to blase;
> So that the Holy Goost gloweth but as a glede
> Til that lele love ligge on hym and blowe.[24]
> And thanne flawmeth he as fir on Fader and on *Filius*
> And melteth hire myght into mercy –

(B XVII 220–9)

The *unkynde creatures* lack the *lele love* necessary to call forth the merciful action of the Holy Ghost – not surprisingly in view of their desire to destroy 'lele love or lif'. To be *unkynde* is to lack love, and this is corroborated by the citation of *Si linguis hominum loquar* a little further on (B XVII 260a) following a discussion of how *unkyndenesse* quenches the Holy Ghost, which plainly identifies *unkyndenesse* with the lack of *caritas* of which St. Paul speaks in I *Corinthians* 13.

The *caritas* the *unkynde creatures* lack is equated with mercy as the Samaritan continues:

> So grace of the Holy Goost the greet myght of the Trinite
> Melteth to mercy – to merciable and to noon othere.

(B XVII 232–3)

The Samaritan presents the proper action of the Holy Ghost as very much to do with mercy, and the equation between love and mercy on the part of man may be motivated by a desire to stress a correspondence between the actions of those who are *kynde* and those of the Holy Ghost. Perhaps the matter can be stated more strongly: Langland may be suggesting that the *kynde* man partakes of the nature of the Holy Ghost, which is fully expressed only when He is being merciful. Lines which follow shortly seem to point to an identity between the nature of the Holy Ghost and the *kynde* man. The somewhat difficult use of the *kynde* of line 250 (the *kynde* of fire is not self-evidently combustible material) suggests that purposeful play is being made with its relation to the *unkynde* of line 252:

> Ac hewe fir at a flynt foure hundred wynter –
> But thow have tache to take it with, tonder or broches,
> Al thi labour is lost and al thi long travaille;
> For may no fir flaumbe make, faille it his kynde.
> So is the Holy Goost God and grace withouten mercy
> To alle unkynde creatures – Crist hymself witnesseth:
> *Amen dico vobis, nescio vos &c.*

(B XVII 247–52a)

---

[24] C here (XIX 189) reads 'Til þat loue and bileue leliche to hym blowe'. The introduction of *bileue* as a requirement is perhaps in line with the C text's moves to diminish the stature of *kynde wit* (unless we are to suppose that the *kynde* have *bileue*). It may be that Langland came to suppose that his B text treatment of the natural gave insufficient weight to the Christian revelation. But if this is so, the natural still retains great potency in C as it stands (perhaps not fully revised).

*Unkynde*ness, it is suggested, is a failure to have the *kynde* of the fire which is the Holy Ghost: there is nothing for the Holy Ghost to catch in the *unkynde*, nothing in them of the same *kynde* as Himself.

The lines which follow seem to push further the suggestion that *unkynde* men lack an identity of nature with the Holy Ghost:

> Be unkynde to thyn evenecristene, and al that thow kanst bidde –
> Delen and do penaunce day and nyght evere,
> And purchace al the pardon of Pampilon and Rome,
> And indulgences ynowe, and be *ingratus* to thi kynde,
> The Holy Goost hereth thee noght, ne helpe may thee by reson;
> For unkyndenesse quencheth hym, that he kan noght shyne,
> Ne brenne ne blase clere, for blowynge of unkyndenesse.
> Poul the Apostel preveth wheither I lye:
> *Si linguis hominum loquar &c.*
> (B XVII 253–60a)

One suspects that the rather surprising *ingratus* is used to introduce the idea of grace. The suggestion is that to be *ingratus* to one's *kynde* is to be lacking in grace towards them. But *ingratus* here seems to be equivalent to *unkynde*, so that to be *unkynde* is to be the opposite of the Holy Ghost's nature as Grace. The Holy Ghost needs to be blown upon by *lele love* to shine: here there is an identity of nature. Conversely, *unkyndenesse*, opposed as it is to the nature of the Holy Ghost, not surprisingly acts as a negative upon the Holy Ghost's positive – its blowing cancels out His activity.

The Samaritan goes on to envisage the *unkynde* man not in terms of his negative relationship to the fire of the Holy Ghost, but as a torch himself. However, the lines corroborate the suggestion of those shortly preceding that the *unkynde* man lacks the *kynde* of the fire that is the Holy Ghost. The *unkynde* man fails to *blase*:

> Forthi beth war, ye wise men that with the world deleth,
> That riche ben and reson knoweth – ruleth wel youre soule;
> Beth noght unkynde, I conseille yow, to youre evenecristene;
> For manye of yow riche men, by my soule, men telleth,
> Ye brenne, but ye blase noght, and that is a blynd bekene!
> (B XVII 261–5)

The imagery here, elsewhere used of the Holy Ghost, suggests that man is under an obligation, which the *unkynde* man fails to fulfil, to be as the Holy Ghost is in His true and full nature, that is, blazing with a warm and comforting flame of mercy and love.

*Unkyndenesse* in these last lines is essentially the failure to give to those in need, and this becomes explicit in the continuation. Here, too, a return is made to the other form of *unkyndenesse* with which this episode is concerned, murder:

> Dives deyde dampned for his unkyndenesse
> Of his mete and his moneie to men that it nedede.

> Ech a riche, I rede, reward at hym take,
> And gyveth youre good to that God that grace of ariseth.
> For that ben unkynde to hise, hope I noon oother
> But thei dwelle ther Dives is dayes withouten ende.[25]
>     Thus is unkyndenesse the contrarie that quencheth, as it were,
> The grace of the Holy Goost, Goddes owne kynde.
> For that kynde dooth, unkynde fordooth – as thise corsede theves,
> Unkynde Cristene men, for coveitise and envye
> Sleeth a man for his moebles, with mouth or with handes.
> For that the Holy Goost hath to kepe, tho harlotes destruyeth –
> The which is lif and love, the leye of mannes body.
> For every manere good man may be likned to a torche,
> Or ellis to a tapur, to reverence the Trinite;
> And whoso morthereth a good man, me thynketh, by myn inwit,
> He fordooth the levest light that Oure Lord lovyeth.

(B XVII 266–82)

The reciprocity of *kynde*ness and God's grace is here made sharply apparent by having the *kynde*ness to the needy recognised as giving to God, 'that grace of ariseth', and that reciprocity helps to draw the *kynde* man and God together, suggesting that they both do essentially the same thing, that is give mercifully. Furthermore, the pun on *kynde* in line 274 (Kynde is the Creator) binds God and man together as the reader holds the two terms of the pun together in his mind; and we are invited to find the activity of the *kynde* man a partaking of the creativity of God in its sustaining of the initial divine gift of life.[26] It is, in fact, very tempting to speak of the *kynde* man as partaking of the nature of God in his giving. Certainly, if to be *unkynde* is to be contrary to the Holy Ghost (and God the Creator – but such distinctions of Person are perhaps not to be attempted in the face of line 273's assertion that the grace of the Holy Ghost is God's *kynde*) the *kynde* man will be in harmony with Him, his activities expressive of His nature. It is perhaps possible to see this spelt out at the beginning of the second paragraph of the passage just quoted. The quenching of the Holy Ghost by *unkyndenesse* is, at one level, the prevention of the operation of the Holy Ghost in mercy towards the *unkynde* man brought about by that man's *unkyndenesse*, which, as we have already seen (the *Thus* marks a recapitulation) acts as a cancelling negative on the Holy Ghost's natural and characteristic behaviour. But it may also be the denial and destruction of the love shown by the *kynde* man, a love which may be considered expressive of the Holy Ghost. Love is said to be the *leye* of a man's body, and the imagery makes the connection with the Holy Ghost, whose proper activity has been likened to a flame. That the *kynde* man does indeed show love is indicated by the fact that the

---

[25] In the C version (XIX 228–49) we are told that Dives won his wealth *riȝtfulliche* and are asked how those who are *unkynde* and yet won their goods falsely will excuse themselves.
[26] Glossing this passage Schmidt (1987), p. 216, draws attention to the ambiguity of the *kynde* in line 274 between human *kynde*ness and God as Kynde. Langland's word-play here seems likely to express what was for him a real relation, not merely a verbal one.

object of the destructive activity of the 'unkynde Cristene men' is love – this is part, it seems, of what *kynde* men do and the *unkynde fordo*.

The equation between the Holy Ghost and the *kynde* man is perhaps enabled further by syntactic ambiguities in lines 277–8. It may be possible to take line 278 as referring to the Holy Ghost, in which case the Holy Ghost becomes constitutive of the man who loves. As earlier Piers described Truth dwelling in the heart, so now man is informed by the divine under a different aspect. It may also be possible to understand the Holy Ghost as the object, rather than the subject, of 'hath to kepe', which again would allow us to see the Holy Ghost as part of the being of the good man.

In any case, man is at least an image of the Trinity, as the last lines of the passage tell us. The love of man is likened to a flame, and whether or not the torch that is the Trinity shows a flame depends upon the activity of the Holy Ghost. It is in virtue of this flame of love that the good man is a true image of the Trinity in its complete nature. But the *unkynde* man is a *blynd bekene*, because he does not love. He is an incomplete image of the Trinity, since he fails to mirror the true nature of the Holy Ghost in a flame of love. We might say that the failure of the *unkynde* man to be a true image of the Trinity is the correlate in the realm of being to his opposition to the Holy Ghost in the realm of action, opposition expressed in his failure to love, to give graciously, and to show mercy.

Haukyn spoke of a cruel *coveitise* obstructing *kyndenesse*. In an extreme form the cruelty of covetousness can end in the *unkynde*ness of murder. Murder, the Samaritan tells us, is the worst sin against the Holy Ghost.

> Ac yet in manye mo maneres men offenden the Holy Goost;
> Ac this is the worste wise that any wight myghte
> Synnen ayein the Seint Spirit – assenten to destruye
> For coveitise of any kynnes thyng that Crist deere boughte.
> How myghte he aske mercy, or any mercy hym helpe,
> That wikkedliche and wilfulliche wolde mercy aniente?
>    Innocence is next God, and nyght and day it crieth
> "Vengeaunce! Vengeaunce! Forgyve be it nevere
> That shente us and shedde oure blood – forschapte us, as it semed:
> *Vindica sanguinem iustorum!*"
> Thus "Vengeaunce, vengeaunce!" verrey charite asketh;
> And sith Holy Chirche and charite chargeth this so soore,
> Leve I nevere that Oure Lord wol love that charite lakketh,
> Ne have pite for any preiere [that he pleyneth ther].
>
> (B XVII 283–95)

Here the need for mercy to be exercised for mercy to be found is reiterated, taking us back to earlier affirmations setting the *unkynde* man against the Holy Ghost. But the passage reveals also that the murderer is set against the other members of the Trinity too, and since murder may be considered only the ultimate point to which the *unkynde*ness that opposes mercy and refuses love tends, it would appear that the *unkynde* man in general is at least in potential opposition to the Trinity in all its Persons (we have already been told that *unkyndenesse* is set against 'Goddes owne kynde' which suggests it will not oppose one Person only). Murder opposes God the Father because it is a *forschaping* of his creation. This point had already been made, in fact, when we were told 'that kynde dooth, unkynde fordooth', since this includes a reference to Kynde the Creator, who gives life to all things – the *unkynde* man seeks to reverse God's creativity. Furthermore, the destruction specifically of love which *unkyndenesse* desires to destroy, and which murder achieves is also an affront to Kynde, who is, as we have seen, associated in His own right with love, actually being identified in the C text as 'love and lif', and whose very creativity may be considered an expression of love.[27] But then, that the *unkynde* man should be set against Kynde is no surprise – his opposition is expressed with great directness at the level of the word which defines him. Finally, the *unkyndenesse* of the murderer is an affront to Christ, because its lack of mercy goes against the mercy Christ showed in the redemption, and the destruction of life murder perpetrates flies in the face of Christ's life-giving activity.

All in all, the Samaritan's speech is a thoroughgoing and multi-faceted condemnation of the unGodliness of the *unkynde* man. *Unkyndenesse* is a fundamental unlovingness which opposes the *kynde* of God Himself; it is perhaps to be seen as a failure to partake of that *kynde* as man should. But the setting of *unkyndenesse* against God's *kynde* is bound to activate, if such activation is required, the sense of 'natural' at least latent in the word *unkyndenesse*: man's *unkyndenesse* is a going against man's *kynde* as well as God's. This is implicit too in the way *unkyndenesse* prevents man being a true image of the Trinity; in doing this it distorts man's nature. But if this is so, the *kynde*ness that seems to align man so closely with God must be understood as a manifestation of man's nature; we may even be justified in saying that simply through being true to his nature man partakes of the nature of God. This idea of a partaking of the divine nature might be set alongside the teachings of mystical theologians, and, indeed, critics have not been reluctant to trace signs of a doctrine of deification in *Piers Plowman*.[28] The *trewe* man was, according to Holy Church 'a god by the gospel', and, as in the last chapter, though now in the light of the Samaritan's speech, rather than in response to the designation of God as Kynde, we may feel a pressure impelling us to adapt her formula, substituting the *kynde* man.

But Langland's confidence in the saving power of man's nature and the

---

[27] A. O. Lovejoy, *The Great Chain of Being* (Cambridge, Mass., 1948), pp. 67–9, shows how neo-platonic thought could suppose that God's creativity was required of him by his nature as Love.

[28] See particularly Vasta (1965); also Bennett (1972), on I 90–1, p. 108; Pearsall (1978) on I 86, p. 46.

natural conditions of existence makes no demand that man's nature should be perfected. And neither is his confidence laid up in the original nature of man as it was before the Fall.[29] The Samaritan's speech ends with a repudiation of *unkyndenesse* that sees it as inexcusable because not proceeding from anything in the evidently imperfect *kynde* of man as he is now or in the natural and often unfortunate conditions of his post-lapsarian existence. Sins that do so proceed will be easily forgiven. The Samaritan presents an allegorical interpretation of the three things that drive a man from his house, a wicked wife, rain on his bed and 'smoke and smolder':

> The wif is oure wikked flessh that wol noght be chastised,
> For kynde clyveth on hym evere to contrarie the soule.
> And though it falle, it fynt skiles, that "Frelete it made,"
> And "That is lightly foryyven and foryeten bothe
> To man that mercy asketh and amende thenketh."
> The reyn that reyneth ther we rest sholde
> Ben siknesses and sorwes that we suffren oughte,
> As Poul the Apostle to the peple taughte:
> *Virtus in infirmitate perficitur.*
> And though that men make muche doel in hir angre,
> And ben inpacient in hir penaunce, pure reson knoweth
> That thei han cause to contrarie, by kynde of hir siknesse;
> And lightliche Oure Lord at hir lyves ende
> Hath mercy on swiche men, that so yvele may suffre.
> Ac the smoke and the smolder that smyt in oure eighen,
> That is coveitise and unkyndenesse, that quencheth Goddes mercy.
> For unkyndenesse is the contrarie of alle kynnes reson;
> For ther nys sik ne sory, ne noon so muche wrecche
> That he ne may lovye, and hym like, and lene of his herte
> Good wille, good word – bothe wisshen and wilnen
> All manere men mercy and foryifnesse,
> And lovye hem lik hymself, and his lif amende.[30]

(B XVII 331–51)

The Samaritan's speech as a whole, we might say, moves from an affirmation of the necessity of love to an affirmation of its sufficiency. And love is not

[29] Augustine well expresses the orthodox position on the relation between man's pre- and post-lapsarian natures:

> Sic etiam ipsam naturam aliter dicimus, cum proprie loquimur, naturam hominis, in qua primum in suo genere inculpabilis factus est: aliter istam, in qua ex illius damnati poena, et mortales et ignari et carni subditi nascimur; juxta quem modum dicit Apostolus, *Fuimus enim et nos filii irae, sicut et caeteri.*

(*De Libero Arbitrio* III 19; PL 32, 1297)

I would suggest that for Langland the bleakness of this view of our nature after the Fall is dissipated by his sense that our nature still remains potently attached to the divine.

[30] Schmidt (1987), pp. 349–50 remarks, 'The skilful use of *kynde* in 332, 341 shows how sins arising from the first two sources [weakness of bodily nature and outward affliction] may find forgiveness while those due to *unkyndenesse* . . . extinguish the fire of God's grace, . . .'

inhibited by anything in the nature or natural conditions of man; only *unkyndenesse* stands in its way. For the Samaritan it is only unnaturalness that will lead us to damnation (and this is perhaps only proper if the tripartite structure of the lines just quoted allows us to associate *unkyndenesse*, contrary to God and to any reasonable motivation, not with the flesh and the world but with the devil, who himself is unable to receive God's mercy[31]). If only we can follow our sinful natures, which still naturally possess the flame of love, so far as to love and give (this is also what the law of *kynde* instructs us to do), we may be assured that our merciful dealing will be reciprocated in the mercy of God towards us. It is, we may feel, a less demanding version of the good life than that which centred on Truth and fulfilling the terms of His pardon.

The mitigation of the regrettable aspects of the nature and natural conditions of man has its positive counterpart in the actually beneficial roles the poem discovers for the sin and suffering that are interwoven in our postlapsarian nature and existence. The positive contribution that sin and suffering are able to make leads, as we have seen, to God's assuming man's *kynde*. It seems very possible that this recognition of the possibilities man's *kynde* offers God because of its very fallen nature may lie behind Langland's sense that the natural, with all its defects, is something crucial to the pursuit of salvation. But it is certainly the case that what is *kynde* for man achieves its greatest potency for salvation in the assumption of man's *kynde* by Christ in the Incarnation. As man, Christ feels the ethical constraints human nature lays upon men. Ultimately, the obligation to love and give to one's fellowmen is grounded in one's blood brotherhood with them. It is a brotherhood Piers feels on the half-acre, when he has starved his idle workers into submission and is worried about the propriety of this procedure:

> [And] it are my blody bretheren, for God boughte us alle.
> Truthe taughte me ones to loven hem ech one
> And to helpen hem of alle thyng, ay as hem nedeth.
>
> (B VI 207–9)

Piers feels, in fact, that he is at risk of being *unkynde* by failing to love and give, obligations he locates in his being of the same nature as other men, sinners though they be. Christ will feel the same bond at the Last Judgement:

> Ac to be merciable to man thanne, my kynde it asketh,
> For we beth bretheren of blood, but noght in baptisme alle.
>
> (B XVIII 376–7)

[31] The order flesh, world, devil is found, for instance, in *The Tretyse of Loue*, p. 119. This same work appears to see the influence of the world as expressed through the suffering to which those in it are subjected (p. 128), rather than through varieties of 'worldliness'.

and again, in a passage the C version of which is fuller on the role of *kynde*:

> And so of alle wykkede y wol here take veniaunce.
> And ȝut my kynde in my kene ire shal constrayne my will –
> *Domine, ne in furore tuo arguas me –*
> To be merciable to monye of my halue-bretherne.
> For bloed may se bloed bothe afurst and acale
> Ac bloed may nat se bloed blede, bote hym rewe.
> *Audivi archana verba, que non licet homini loqui.*
> Ac my rihtwysnesse and rihte shal regnen in helle,
> And mercy al mankynde bifore me in heuene.
> For y were an vnkynde kyng bote y my kyn helpe,
> And namliche at such a nede þat nedes helpe asketh.
> *Non intres in iudicium cum seruo tuo.*[32]

(C XX 434–42a)

Like man, Christ must avoid *unkyndenesse* – and this suggestion that the Deity Himself has to negotiate a passage round *unkyndenesse* makes it appear particularly threatening and heinous. Christ's kinship with man demands that, like any *kynde* man, he should show mercy to his brother man. This can, perhaps, be seen as a somewhat bewildering yet delightful and satisfying transformation of the kindling of the Holy Ghost's mercy by human *kyndenesse*. Divine mercy is stimulated within Christ by the *kyndenesse* to which he is obligated by his *kynde* as man. The natural achieves the fullest power to save, yet without the least hint of Pelagianism, the suspicion of which I have suggested may be bound up with *kynde wit*'s failure to carry Langland's aspirations for the natural. What is even more remarkable, the human and natural achieves a constraining power over the divine. Yet it is also God's nature as God that requires him to be *kynde*, for the Samaritan has told us that to be *unkynde* is to run contrary to that nature.[33] More than

---

[32] One might compare the following passage from *The South English Legendary*, ed. Charlotte D'Evelyn and Anna J. Mill *EETS* 235 (London, 1956) p. 225, lines 130–2:

> Wel þou wost þat sunfol men . gret loue he cudde ofte
> For he was ibore of sunfol men . & for ȝam to deþe ido
> He mot nede to ȝam be[o] milde . for riȝt kunde it wolde so

As with the Langland passage, it is possible that the obligation arises not solely out of kinship (in Langland there may be a sense that Christ is obligated not only as kinsman, but also as king; here Christ may be naturally urged to mildness by what he has already done for man), but kinship and the natural bonds it creates are plainly crucial.

[33] There would seem to be an impropriety at the verbal level in God, who is Kynde, being *unkynde*, but this seems likely to be matched by a more substantial impropriety: God would be thwarting his own creative purposes were he *unkynde* enough to allow mankind to be damned, since man has been made with a view to something other than damnation. Again, *unkyndenesse* would, as we have seen, involve a lack of love, but God is Love and would have to contradict his own nature to be *unkynde* (Kynde is identified as love at C X 168–9). It seems to me that this sort of consideration brings Langland perilously (from an orthodox point of view) close to the doctrine of universal salvation. This is another point of similarity with Julian of Norwich, who seems worried about the failure of her vision to show her any damned human beings.

ever this God obligated to be *kynde* by his *kynde* as both man and God seems fittingly called Kynde.

At the end of the poem Langland reformulates Piers' pardon as *redde quod debes*, and in being *kynde* to man God, as it were, *reddit quod debet*. Here, it would seem, God's mercy and his justice are reconciled, since justice is a matter of rendering people what one owes them.[34] In man's case, to be *kynde* may be to fulfil the demand of the pardon, *redde quod debes*. We should remember that justice is susceptible of being understood as the fulfilment of the demands of the Gospel as these relate to our fellow men.[35] To be just, in this understanding, is to be loving. Conscience himself, as the following passage shows, seems to understand the essential content of *redde quod debes* as the forgiveness of others, which is, in fact, an act of mercy and love, a being *kynde* to one's fellows. And this mercy and love on our part, so the citation from the Paternoster suggests, will be met with the merciful forgiveness of our own sins by God. The situation recalls the Samaritan's discourse on *unkyndenesse* which stresses how human mercy is required to call forth God's mercy. Conscience explains how Grace provided the Eucharistic bread for

> '. . . tho that hadde ypaied
> To Piers pardon the Plowman, *redde quod debes.*'
>    'How?' quod al the comune. 'Thow conseillest us to yelde
> Al that we owen any wight er we go to housel?'
>    'That is my conseil,' quod Conscience, 'and Cardinale Vertues;
> That ech man foryyve oother, and that wole the Paternoster –
> *Et dimitte nobis debita nostra &c.* –
> And so to ben assoilled, and siththen ben houseled.'
>    'Ye? Baw!' quod a brewere, 'I wole noght be ruled,
> By Jesu! for al youre janglynge, with *Spiritus Iusticie*, . . .'
>
> (B XIX 392–400)

I suggested in the last chapter that the change of God's name from Truth to Kynde had to do with a movement away from an impossibly difficult moral injunction to something more adapted to man's capabilities. If we understand *redde quod debes* as essentially an injunction to be merciful and loving, to be *kynde*, in fact[36] (and it is worth noting that the Cardinal Virtues, natural virtues,[37] urge *redde quod debes*), we can align the change of text in

---

[34] See Aquinas, *Summa Theologica* II II q. 58, a. 11., 'proprius actus iustitiae nihil aliud est quam reddere unicuique quod suum est.'

[35] See Kean (1964), p. 256.

[36] See Frank (1957), pp. 107ff. for such an understanding of *redde quod debes*. Frank supposes that love of God is included in the injunction. This is not evident in what Conscience says in the passage just quoted, but in any case Langland would probably have regarded love of God as a part of being *kynde*. At C XVII 151ff. Liberum Arbitrium concedes that *Sarresynes* may love God 'as by lawe of kynde', since for the creature to honour his creator is 'kyndly thyng'. Indeed, B XVII 268ff. suggests that to be *kynde* to one's fellow-men is to be *kynde* to God Himself.

[37] See, however, Chapter 1, notes 77 and 79.

Piers' pardon with the change of names for God, and see both of them as making an accommodation with the *kynde* of man[38] and, more positively, as exalting it to the highest places in the moral and metaphysical schemes of things. But that exaltation is only appropriate, since *kynde* is so powerful and benign a concept. Morally, it becomes the place of reconciliation for mercy and justice, for law and love; metaphysically, it proclaims the nature of man and of God, as God and as Man, displaying them as, essentially, Love, and through it suggestions arise concerning an essential unity of human and divine.

[38] It is worth pointing out that taken literally the injunction *redde quod debes* appears easier to achieve than Dowel, since it implies the possibility of its own fulfilment in a way in which the naked command to do well does not. If a man is to give *back* what he *owes*, it implies that he, at least at one stage, had it to give back.

# Conclusion

The doggedness that apparently kept Langland at work on *Piers Plowman* for a quarter of a century, permitting the rescue of the poem from successive crises and breakdowns, can be seen in operation in his dealings with the *kynde*. The natural offers itself in several shapes which, for one reason or another, will not do; but the idea cannot be abandoned because both about it and through it, Langland knows, central affirmations are to be made. I have argued that Langland comes to see large inadequacies in *kynde wit* which turns out not to be the shape in which the idea of the natural can be best celebrated and in which it can be made expressive of the deepest truths, and have suggested that its inadequacy has to do with its being tied in several ways to the merely human and natural, rather than to the divine. However, if we can understand what Will learns from Kynde in Passus B XX as a variety of *kynde wit*, we might note how in this its most plausible form *kynde wit* arises out of an undergoing of the will of God and see here a development of the concept of *kynde wit* which is in line with a larger movement in the poem as a whole. For it seems to me that *Piers Plowman* becomes increasingly a poem that celebrates God's activity rather than man's.[1]

Perhaps more easily than is the case with *kynde wit*, which must tend to appear as an instrument of moral endeavour belonging to man, the idea of *kynde*ness can accommodate a sense that the important activity is God's. The presentation of *kynde*ness in B XVII makes it clear that being *kynde* is only a qualification for the mercy of God, of which, in any case, it is an image: at the end of the Passus being *kynde* involves being sinful – man's need for the activity of God is clearly evident. Further, the drift of the passage is to see the essential performance on man's part as the avoidance of *unkyndenesse* – an avoidance that ought to be achievable with some ease since the committing of *unkyndenesse* is unnatural. To avoid what is unnatural seems to be doubly passive, since one's nature bears one away from unnaturalness automatically. We seem to be at some distance from the

[1] The emergence of Patience as a figure of authority is an important indicator of the movement away from a concentration on man's activity; the stress laid on the redemptive activity of Christ, towards which the poem presses, and the according of a highly significant role to the Holy Spirit as Grace at the end of the poem are aspects of the increasing concentration on what God does for man's salvation.

active heroics of a journey to Truth, the deliberate pursuit of a goal towards which one is directed by one's *kynde wit*.

There is a connection between passivity and suffering, and it is noticeable that the idea of *kynde*ness for Langland accommodates suffering and the sin which is ultimately its cause: there is a recognition that these elements of human experience are as *kynde* as man's impulses to charity, but this is not permitted to invalidate the ideal of *kynde*ness. This accommodation of the negative elements of the natural is evident too in the development of the figure Kynde, whose love is eventually affirmed out of a full recognition of its hiddenness. The accommodation of the negative within the idea of the natural increases that idea's potency: because the difficult issues are not evaded, the celebration of the natural in which they have been acknowledged is much more powerful than would otherwise be the case.

The acceptance of the negative aspects of the natural is perhaps a prerequisite for an approximation of the natural to the divine, for it means that those aspects do not constitute a scandal standing in the way of such a manoeuvre. Certainly, in its manifestations as *kynde*ness and Kynde, the natural is closely linked to the divine, indeed becomes an expression of it. We can speak in terms of a divinisation of the natural through which the natural achieves its highest dignity.[2]

The accommodation of the negative within the ideal of *kynde* is, I think, a crucial difference between Langland on the one hand and Chaucer and Gower on the other over the question of the moral status of the natural. Chaucer and Gower seem to be very sympathetic to the idea of the natural as a force for good, and yet in the end neither of them is able to sustain such an understanding of the natural: for instance, there does not seem to me to be much credibility left to the high moral claims made for natural sexual love in *Troilus and Criseyde* at the end of that poem, whilst the reconciliation between sexuality and morality Gower is continually attempting in *Confessio Amantis* is finally made to appear impossible.[3] Troilus can think in terms of a continuum between human sexual love and the love that rules the universe, but the action of the poem and the remarks made by the narrator at its conclusion put considerable pressure on that position.[4] Both Chaucer and Gower have ultimately to acknowledge that sexuality is not directed towards the divine and so are unable to offer a divinisation of the natural as Langland

[2] One can also see an approximation of natural and divine with respect to *kynde wit*. What Will learns at the end of the poem after undergoing the natural process of ageing is taught him by Kynde, who is God: the wisdom is thus both natural and divine. Again, some of God's knowledge is obtained by undergoing natural human experience, so that divine knowledge is in part *kynde wit* (see B XVIII 217–24).

[3] For narratorial claims about love in *Troilus and Criseyde* see I 211–59; I 1079–85; III 1786–1806. At *Confessio Amantis* VIII 2130ff. Genius makes it clear that Love and Reason are principles essentially opposed.

[4] See Troilus at III 1744–71 (also III 1261) and the narrator at V 1828ff. It is very likely Troilus himself who condemns love as 'blynde lust' (V 1824) just before the narrator's final comments.

can. For a sense among Langland's contemporaries of the positive nature of the worldly, with all its limitations and unsatisfactorinesses, we have to go, I think, to the Pearl-poet and to Julian of Norwich. Both honour the opportunities offered by an exposure to the negative aspects of the world, the Pearl-poet by suggesting that the relation of moral failure to moral success is by no means simply one of exclusion and also by hinting that a guilty human perspective ultimately reveals more of the nature of God than that of an innocent,[5] Julian (in part) by offering us the figure of the Son returning from his experiences of the world in a garment of superior beauty to that available to the Godhead before.[6] Langland, rather like Julian, suggests that the Incarnation, His involvement in the suffering of sinful man, actually makes a difference to God, and it is this that most powerfully validates the natural.

Langland strongly endorses the doctrine of the *felix culpa*, the fortunateness of which, for him, extends right into the nature of God Himself. Fallen experience is crucial in the attaining of human wisdom, but it is also crucial for the maintaining of divine omniscience, and the Incarnation, an act which the Fall elicits, is presented as the factor that determines that God shall be merciful towards man. It is no surprise, then, that the end of the poem should find Conscience enthusiastically embracing another journey into a dangerous and sinful world, with no hint of nostalgia for the enclosed place of protective goodness which has just been penetrated by the forces of evil. The tone at the end of *Piers Plowman* differs most interestingly from that at the end of another great religious poem which shares areas of interest with Langland's work, *Paradise Lost*. In the later poem another place of goodness (a place which offers protection, one might say in retrospect, from the unpleasantnesses of fallen existence) has to be abandoned. In Milton's poem the sense of loss is acute, and one wonders just in what way Milton assents to the *felix culpa*.[7] His separatist treatment of the Father and the Son makes it impossible to realise compellingly a sense that at the highest point of the universe sin has a real and positive contribution to make. It may be that a reluctance really to believe in the positive value of fallen experience governs the form Milton's poem takes – it offers itself as a beautifully ordered

---

[5] For substantiation of these remarks see Hugh White, 'Blood in *Pearl*', *RES*, n.s. 38 (1987), 1–13.

[6] *A Book of Showings* p. 543.

[7] For a discussion of the doctrine of the *felix culpa* in Milton see 'Milton and the Paradox of the Fortunate Fall' in A. O. Lovejoy's *Essays in the History of Ideas* (Baltimore, 1948), 277–95. Lovejoy notes that St. Francis de Sales brings out more pointedly than Milton 'the strangest aspect of the paradox', God's *need* for a fallen race to evoke fully the divine attributes and powers (p. 294). I suspect Langland may be even more startling than de Sales, but Lovejoy's comment already indicates that Milton is not mobilising the full power of the paradox (perhaps, one might suggest, because his commitment to it is not as wholehearted as it might be). In his *Paradise Lost* (London, 1980) G. K. Hunter registers a *caveat* against using the *felix culpa* too simply as a lens through which to view Milton's poem: as we read it, we do not feel it to be a Divine Comedy, but respond to much of what happens as tragedy (pp. 24f.).

structure, which one might claim is a nostalgic imitation of the unfallen: the fracturedness of Langland's poem stands in marked contrast. One aspect of the order of *Paradise Lost* is its symmetry about a mid-point which, perhaps significantly, is the crucial event in the ejection of evil from heaven, rather than something connected with the creation of man or the bringing of good out of evil through Messiah's redemptive sacrifice:[8] at the centre of Milton's poem is the clear separation of good and evil, whilst Langland's concept of *kynde* is one that permits a co-existence of good and evil, an interinvolvement, indeed. One can also see a contrast between Milton's worry about failing to express things correctly[9] and Langland's method of developing his poem out of recognitions that he has got things wrong: one could say that the development of *Piers Plowman* enacted the *felix culpa*. Certainly the journey into an imperfect world at the end of *Piers Plowman* is more straightforwardly embraced than that at the end of *Paradise Lost*. Conscience focuses his future experience unequivocally on the redemptive figure of Piers, rather than on the ambivalent 'world' which Milton offers Adam and Eve.[10] And besides this, there is in Milton's ending the nostalgia to which I have referred. The forward movement out of Paradise and into history competes with a backward perspective reinforced by the structure of the poem which folds it onto itself, returning it to the mid-point where Messiah separates good and evil. Through its backward gestures *Paradise Lost* invites us back into itself to indulge a regret for the passing of moral simplicity and moral power (as well as for a paradisal mode of experience), whereas *Piers Plowman* thrusts us out, unsparingly and exhilaratingly, into pursuit of Piers in a realm beyond the poem, which the poem has told us is a realm of moral confusion, unclarity, arduous endeavour and moral weakness – indeed it has partaken itself of all those aspects of the fallen realm[11] rather than offering an environ-

---

[8] At the mid-point of the poem by line count in the first edition, Messiah ascends his chariot to drive the fallen angels out of heaven. For comment on this and on the mirror-symmetry of the poem about this mid-point see *The Poems of John Milton*, ed. John Carey and Alastair Fowler (London, 1968), p. 441–3.

[9] See III 1ff.; VII 12–20, 38–9; IX 20–1, 41ff. and also what Raphael says at V 563–76. In the Invocations Milton tends to deny his fallen human responsibility for the poem, seeking to present it as the word of God. Langland clearly is not interested in this strategy: indeed, he allows the view that his poem is a whimsical obsession which only distracts the author from truly important endeavours (see B XII 10ff.).

[10] XII 646.

[11] To claim that the poem partakes of moral weakness might not seem justified. But I think we might regard the expression of a deterministic view of salvation where the A text breaks down as evidence of surrender in the face of the difficulties of articulating what Dowel, Dobet and Dobest are: on the view expressed by Will at this point one may as well give up trying to teach people about morality since it will not make any difference to their ultimate destination. And in general, Will's argumentative tendency could be understood as a manifestation of the *poem's* impatience, and what can be viewed as a heroic refusal to rest content with unsatisfactory answers may also appear a bad-tempered inquisition into matters that need not be probed. It seems possible that Langland, at least at times, felt the writing of the poem might be a sinful self-indulgence (see note 9).

ment in which a yearning for simplicity and power can be indulged. It is, I think, in large measure because the poem has found out how to substantiate its trust in the natural that it can project us into fallen reality so exuberantly.

# Bibliography

*Editions of Piers Plowman*

*The Vision of William concerning Piers the Plowman, in Three Parallel Texts*, ed. W. W. Skeat (Oxford, 1886, repr. 1954)

*Piers Plowman: A Critical Edition of the A-Version*, ed. Thomas A. Knott and David C. Fowler (Baltimore, 1952)

*Piers Plowman*, The A Version, ed. George Kane (London, 1960)

*Piers Plowman: The Prologue and Passus I–VII of the B text*, ed. J. A. W. Bennett (Oxford, 1972)

*Piers Plowman: The B Version*, ed. George Kane and E. Talbot Donaldson (London, 1975)

*The Vision of Piers Plowman, A Complete Edition of the B-Text*, New Edition, ed. A. V. C. Schmidt (London, 1987)

*Piers Plowman, An Edition of the C-Text*, ed. Derek Pearsall (London, 1978)

*Piers Plowman: The Z Version*, ed. A. G. Rigg and Charlotte Brewer (Toronto, 1983)

*Other Primary Texts*

Alan of Lille *Anticlaudianus*, ed. R. Bossuat (Paris, 1955)

Alan of Lille *De Planctu Naturae*, ed. N. Häring, *Studi Medievali*, 19 (1978), 797–879

Alan of Lille *Liber in Distinctionibus Dictionum Theologicalium (Distinctiones) PL* 210, 686–1011

Alan of Lille *Liber Parabolarum PL* 210, 579–94

Aquinas, Thomas *Summa Theologica* Vols. 4–12 (1888–1906) of the Leonine edition of the *Opera*

Azo *Summa Institutionum* (Basel, 1563)

Augustine of Hippo *Contra Epistolam Manichaei PL* 42, 173–206

Augustine of Hippo *De Libero Arbitrio PL* 32, 1221–1310

Boethius *De Consolatione Philosophiae* (*The Consolation of Philosophy*) 2nd Loeb edition (London/Cambridge, Mass., 1973)

Chaucer, Geoffrey *Works*, ed. F. N. Robinson, 2nd ed. (London, 1957)

Cicero *De Republica & De Legibus* (for *Somnium Scipionis*) Loeb edition (London/New York, 1928)

*Corpus Iuris Civilis*, Vol. 1 (*Digest* and *Institutes*) ed. P. Krueger and T. Mommsen, 16th ed. (Berlin, 1954)

*Dives and Pauper*, Vol. 1, ed. P. H. Barnum, *EETS* 275, 280 (Oxford, 1976, 1980)

Gower, John *Confessio Amantis*, ed. G. C. Macaulay, *EETS* e.s. 81, 82 (London, 1900–1)

Gratian *Decretum* in *Corpus Iuris Canonici*, Vol. 1, ed. A. Friedberg (Leipzig, 1879)

Guillaume de Lorris and Jean de Meun *Le Roman de la Rose*, ed. Félix Lecoy (Paris, 1965–70)

Jean de Hautville (Johannes de Hauvilla) *Architrenius*, ed. P. G. Schmidt (München, 1974)

John of Salisbury *Policraticus*, ed. C. C. J. Webb (Oxford, 1909)

Julian of Norwich *A Book of Showings to the Anchoress Julian of Norwich*, ed. E. Colledge and J. Walsh (Toronto, 1978)

*Middle English Sermons*, ed. W. O. Ross, *EETS* o.s. 209 (London, 1940)

Milton, John *Poems*, ed. John Carey and Alastair Fowler (London, 1968)

*Northern Homily Cycle, The*, ed. Saara Nevanlinna, *Mémoires de la Société Néophilologique de Helsinki*, 38, 41 (1972, 1973)

*Renart le Contrefait*, ed. G. Raynaud and H. Lemaître (Paris, 1914)

Richard of St Victor *Benjamin Major*, *PL* 196, 63–202

*South English Legendary, The*, ed. Charlotte d'Evelyn and Anna J. Mill *EETS* 235, 236, 244 (London, 1956, 1959)

*Tretyse of Loue, The*, ed. John H. Fisher, *EETS* o.s. 223 (London, 1951)

*Vices and Virtues, The Book of*, ed. W. N. Francis *EETS* o.s. 217 (London, 1942)

Vincent of Beauvais *Speculum Maius* (Venice, 1591)

Virgil *Opera*, ed. R. A. B. Mynors (Oxford, 1969)

Wyclif, John (attributed) *Select English Works of John Wyclif*, ed. Thomas Arnold (Oxford, 1869–71)

## Critical Literature

Adams, Robert 'The Nature of Need in "Piers Plowman" XX', *Traditio*, 34 (1978), 273–302

Adams, Robert 'Piers' Pardon and Langland's Semi-Pelagianism', *Traditio*, 39 (1983), 367–418

Baker, Denise N. 'From Plowing to Penitence: *Piers Plowman* and 14th century Theology', *Speculum*, 55 (1980), 715–25

Baker, Denise N. 'The Pardons of *Piers Plowman*', *Neuphilologische Mitteilungen*, 85 (1984), 462–72

Baldwin, Anna *The Theme of Government in Piers Plowman* (Cambridge, 1981)

Barr, Helen 'The Use of Latin Quotations in *Piers Plowman* with special reference to Passus XVIII of the "B" Text', *N&Q*, n.s. 33 (1986), 440–8

Bartholomew, B. *Fortuna and Natura: A Reading of Three Chaucer Narratives* (The Hague, 1966)

Bennett, J. A. W. (ed.) *Piers Plowman: The Prologue and Passus I–VII of the B text* (Oxford, 1972)

Bloomfield, M. W. Review of *Piers Plowman and Scriptural Tradition* by D. W. Robertson, Jr and B. F. Huppé, *Speculum*, 27 (1952), 245–9

Bloomfield, M. W. *Piers Plowman as a Fourteenth Century Apocalypse* (New Brunswick, 1961)

Burrow, J. A. 'The Action of Langland's Second Vision', *Essays in Criticism*, 15 (1965), 247–68

Carlyle, R. W. and A. J. *A History of Medieval Political Theory in the West* (Edinburgh/London, 1903–36)

Carey, John and Fowler, Alastair (ed.) *The Poems of John Milton* (London, 1968)

Cohn, Norman *The Pursuit of the Millenium* (London, 1970)

Coleman, Janet *Piers Plowman and the Moderni* (Roma, 1981)

Colledge, E. and Walsh, J. (ed.) *A Book of Showings to the Anchoress Julian of Norwich* (Toronto, 1978)

Copleston, F. C. *Aquinas* (Harmondsworth, 1955)

Davlin, Mary C. '*Kynde Knowyng* as a Major Theme in *Piers Plowman* B', *RES*, n.s. 22 (1971), 1–19

Davlin, Mary C. '*Kynde Knowyng* as a Middle English Equivalent for 'Wisdom' in *Piers Plowman* B', *MAE*, 50 (1981), 5–17

Delhaye, P. *Permanence du Droit Naturel* Analecta Mediaevalia Namur-censia 10 (Louvain/Lille/Montreal, 1960)

D'Entrèves, A. P. *The Medieval Contribution to Political Thought* (Oxford, 1939)

Donaldson, E. Talbot *Piers Plowman: The C-Text and its Poet* (New Haven, 1949)

Dunning, T. P. *Piers Plowman: An Interpretation of the A-Text*, 1st ed. (London, 1937)

Dunning, T. P. *Piers Plowman: An Interpretation of the A-Text*, 2nd ed., revised and edited by T. P. Dolan (Oxford, 1980)

Dunning, T. P. 'Langland and the Salvation of the Heathen', *MAE*, 12 (1943), 45–54

Economou, George D. *The Goddess Natura in Medieval Literature* (Cambridge, Mass., 1972)

Erzgräber, Willi *William Langlands 'Piers Plowman' (Eine Interpretation des C-Textes)* Frankfurter Arbeiten aus dem Gebiete der Anglistik und der Amerika-Studien 3 (Heidelberg, 1957)

Ferguson, Arthur B. *The Articulate Citizen and the English Renaissance* (Durham, N.C., 1965)

Frank, Robert Worth Jr *Piers Plowman and the Scheme of Salvation* (New Haven, 1957)

Gierke, Otto *Political Theories of the Middle Age*, trans. F. W. Maitland (Cambridge, 1900)

Godden, M. R. 'Plowmen and Hermits in Langland's *Piers Plowman*', *RES*, n.s. 35 (1984), 129–63

Goldsmith, Margaret E. *The Figure of Piers Plowman* (Cambridge, 1981)

Gordon, Ida L. *The Double Sorrow of Troilus: A Study of Ambiguities in Troilus and Criseyde* (Oxford, 1970)

Gradon, Pamela 'Langland and the Ideology of Dissent', *PBA*, 66 (1980), 179–205

Gradon, Pamela '*Trajanus Redivivus*: Another look at Trajan in *Piers Plowman*' in *Middle English Studies presented to Norman Davis*, ed. Douglas Gray and E. G. Stanley (Oxford, 1983), 93–114

Gregory, Tullio *Anima Mundi, La filosofia di Guglielmo di Conches e la scuola di Chartres* (Firenze, 1955)

Gregory, Tullio *Platonismo Medievale* (Roma, 1958)

Harwood, Britton J. 'Langland's *Kynde Wit*', *JEGP*, 75 (1976), 330–6

Harwood, Britton J. 'Langland's *Kynde Knowyng* and the Quest for Christ', *MP*, 80 (1983), 242–55

Hort, Greta *Piers Plowman and Contemporary Religious Thought* (London, 1938)

Hunter, G. K. *Paradise Lost* (London, 1980)

Huppé, Bernard F. '*Petrus id est Christus*: Word Play in *Piers Plowman*, The B-Text', *ELH*, 17 (1950), 163–90

Jones, H. S. V. 'Imaginatif in Piers Plowman', *JEGP*, 13 (1914), 583–8

Kane, George and Donaldson, E. Talbot (ed.) *Piers Plowman: The B Version* (London, 1975)

Kean, P. M. 'Love, Law, and *Lewte* in *Piers Plowman*, *RES*, n.s. 15 (1964), 241–61

Kirk, E. D. *The Dream Thought of Piers Plowman* (New Haven, 1972)

Knowlton, E. C. 'Nature in Middle English', *JEGP*, 20 (1921), 186–207

Lawlor, John *Piers Plowman, An Essay in Criticism* (London, 1963)

Lewis, C. S. *Studies in Words* (Cambridge, 1960)

Longo, Joseph A. '*Piers Plowman* and the Tropological Matrix: Passus XI and XII', *Anglia* 82 (1964), 291–308

Lottin, O. *Psychologie et Morale au XII et XIII siècles* (Louvain/Gembloux, 1942–60)

Lovejoy, A. O. *The Great Chain of Being* (Cambridge, Mass., 1948)

Lovejoy, A. O. *Essays in the History of Ideas* (Baltimore, 1948)

Lucks, H. A. 'Natura Naturans – Natura Naturata', *The New Scholasticism*, 9 (1935), 1–24

Mann, Jill 'Eating and Drinking in "Piers Plowman"', *Essays and Studies*, n.s. 32 (1979), 24–43

Martin, Priscilla *Piers Plowman: the Field and the Tower* (London, 1979)

Norton-Smith, John *William Langland* (London, 1980)

Onclin, W. 'Le droit naturel selon les romanistes des XIIe et XIIIe siècles' in *Miscellanea Moralia in honorem eximii domini Arthur Janssen*, Vol. 2 (Louvain/Gembloux, 1949), 329–37

Owen, Dorothy L. *Piers Plowman, A Comparison with some Earlier and Contemporary French Allegories* (London, 1912)

Pearsall, Derek (ed.) *Piers Plowman, An Edition of the C-Text* (London, 1978)

Potts, Timothy C. *Conscience in Medieval Philosophy* (Cambridge, 1980)

Potts, Timothy C. 'Conscience' in *The Cambridge History of Later Medieval Philosophy*, ed. N. Kretzmann, A. Kenny and J. Pimborg (Cambridge, 1982), 687–704

Quirk, Randolph 'Langland's Use of *Kind Wit* and *Inwit*', *JEGP*, 52 (1953), 182–8

Robertson, D. W., Jr and Huppé, B. F. *Piers Plowman and Scriptural Tradition* (Princeton, 1951)

Russell, G. H. 'The Salvation of the Heathen: The Exploration of a Theme in *Piers Plowman*', *Journal of the Warburg and Courtauld Institutes*, 29 (1966), 101–16

Schmidt, A. V. C. 'Langland and the Mystical Tradition' in *The Medieval Mystical Tradition in England*, ed. Marion Glasscoe (Exeter, 1980), 17–38

Schmidt, A. V. C. '*Lele Wordes* and *Bele Paroles*: Some Aspects of Langland's Word-Play', *RES*, n.s. 34 (1983), 137–50

Schmidt, A. V. C. 'The Inner Dreams of *Piers Plowman*', *MAE*, 55 (1986), 24–40

Schmidt, A. V. C. (ed.) *The Vision of Piers Plowman, A Complete Edition of the B-Text*, New Edition (London, 1987)

Scroeder, Mary C. 'The Character of Conscience in *Piers Plowman*', *SP*, 67 (1970), 13–30

Siebeck, H. 'Ueber die Enstehung der Termini natura naturans und natura naturata', *Archiv für Geschichte der Philosophie*, 3 (1890), 370–8

Simpson, James 'From Reason to Affective Knowledge: Modes of Thought and Poetic Form in *Piers Plowman*', *MAE*, 55 (1986), 1–23

Southern, R. W. *Medieval Humanism and Other Studies* (Oxford, 1970)

Stock, Brian *Myth and Science in the Twelfth Century, A Study of Bernard Silvester* (Princeton, 1972)

Stokes, Myra *Justice and Mercy in Piers Plowman* (London/Canberra, 1984)

Tavormina, M. T. ' "Bothe two ben goode": Marriage and Virginity in *Piers Plowman* C 18. 68–100', *JEGP*, 81 (1982), 320–30

Tierney, Brian '*Natura, id est Deus*: A Case of Juristic Pantheism?', *Journal of the History of Ideas*, 24 (1963), 307–22

Tolkien, J. R. R. *A Middle English Vocabulary* (Glossary to *Fourteenth Century Verse and Prose*, ed. K. Sisam) (Oxford, 1922)

Tristram, Phillipa *Figures of Life and Death in Medieval English Literature* (London, 1976)

Vacant, A. and Mangenot E. (ed.) *Dictionnaire de Théologie Catholique* (Paris, 1903–72)

Vasta, E. *The Spiritual Basis of Piers Plowman* (The Hague, 1965)

Verbecke, G. 'L'Influence du Stoicisme sur la Pensée Mediévale en Occident' in *Actas del 5 Congreso Internacional de Filosofía Medieval* (Madrid, 1979), 95–109

Weijers, O. 'Contribution à l'histoire des termes "natura naturans" et "natura naturata" ', *Vivarium*, 16 (1978), 70–80

Wetherbee, W. *Platonism and Poetry in the Twelfth Century* (Princeton, 1972)

Whatley, G. '*Piers Plowman* B 12.277–94: Notes on Language, Text, and Theology', *MP*, 81 (1984), 1–12

Whatley, G. 'The Uses of Hagiography: The Legend of Pope Gregory and the Emperor Trajan in the Middle Ages', *Viator*, 15 (1984), 25–63

White, Hugh 'Langland's Ymaginatif, Kynde and the *Benjamin Major*', *MAE*, 55 (1986), 241–8

White, Hugh 'Blood in *Pearl*', *RES*, n.s. 38 (1987), 1–13

Wittig, J. S. ' "Piers Plowman B", Passus IX–XII: Elements in the Design of the Inward Journey', *Traditio*, 28 (1972), 211–80

# Index

(Personifications from *Piers Plowman* and the concepts they represent generally have a single entry)